MEGATRENDS

- & -

VOLUNTEERISM

by

Sue Vineyard, C.V.M.

Published by
Heritage Arts Publishing, a division of VMSystems

Cover Design & Text Graphics by
Scott T. Hoffman

c. Sue Vineyard, 1993.
ISBN # 0-911029-43-5

Published by:

Heritage Arts Publishing
1807 Prairie Ave.
Downers Grove, IL 60515
(708) 964-1194

Other Books by Sue Vineyard:

Finding Your Way Through The Maze of Volunteer Management*, 1981.
Fund Raising for Hospices.* 1983. (with Judi Lund)
Beyond Banquets, Plaques & Pins: Creative Recognition. Rev. 1989.
Marketing Magic for Volunteer Programs. 1984.
101 Ideas for Volunteer Programs. 1986. (with Steve McCurley)
101 Ways to Raise Resources. 1987. (with Steve McCurley)
How to Take Care of You. Rev. 1989.
Evaluating Volunteers, Programs & Events. 1988.
101 Tips for Volunteer Recruitment. 1988. (with Steve McCurley)
Resource Directory for Volunteer Programs*.1989, 1990. (w/S. McCurley)
The Great Trainer's Guide. 1990.
Secrets of Motivation. 1991.
Secrets of Leadership. 1991. (with Rick Lynch)
Managing Volunteer Diversity. 1992. (with Steve McCurley)

*no longer available

Other Products by Sue Vineyard:

"Care for the Caregiver" (audio)
"Preventing Burnout" (audio)
"Building A Bridge From Dream To Reality: Basic Volunteer Management"
(video)
"Basic Volunteer Management" (Training Kit)

"GRAPEVINE: Volunteerism's Newsletter" (16 p. Newsletter, bi-monthly)
"Grapevine EXTRA" (newsletter update, bi-monthly

Cover & Text design by Scott T. Hoffman using QuarkXPRESS
software on Macintosh Centris 650

TABLE OF CONTENTS

1   *Preface*

3   *Introduction*

9   *Chapter 1:*   Volunteer Community and National Service

33   *Chapter 2:*   Cultural Diversity Within the Ranks of Volunteerism

51   *Chapter 3:*   Growth of Entrepreneurial and Grassroots Volunteering

65   *Chapter 4:*   The Emergence of a National Leadership Group

81   *Chapter 5:*   International Expansion and Inclusion

89   *Chapter 6:*   Ethics and Public Perception

107   *Chapter 7:*   Building Community: Focus on Organization, Capacity and Networking

129   *Chapter 8:*   Expanded Expertise

155   *Chapter 9:*   Professional Improvement & Expanded Sphere of Influence

179   *Chapter 10:*   Changing Roles of Volunteer Program Executives

Addenda:

Bibliography
Books, Products
"GRAPEVINE" order form

Dedicated to those for whom the future awaits:

Bill & Bob Vineyard
Kerri & Filip Vermeylen
Kevin Jacobson
Andrea & Dale Mitchell
Meridith & Bryce Kasper

...and those others they will draw into our family's circle of tomorrow.

"No one can predict to what heights you can soar.
Even you will not know until you spread your wings."

"Chance favors the prepared mind."

****

Many thanks to three people who took time from their busy schedules to review each chapter and respond to my hysterical requests to rush their edits back to me so I could make the book's various deadlines. As usual, their input made this work better and this author is eternally grateful for their continuing support.

Hats off, therefore, to Betty Greer, Director of Volunteer Services at Rex Hospital in Raleigh, NC; Billie Ann Myers, Director, Arkansas Division of Volunteer Services, and Steve McCurley, Partner and the "M" in VMSystems. I thank you all!

PREFACE

When I began to work on this book, I first gathered as many resources as my family room table could hold, that offered any insight into trends that surround us.

As I began to actually write the copy, I carefully put footnotes on every conclusion I had drawn, so that readers might know how I came to think as I did, and to identify my sources.

The more I read, the more I had to go back to what I'd written, to add the increasing number of authors and articles mentioning the same trend I was addressing. By the time I'd written the first chapter's draft, almost every paragraph had at least one footnote, and the footnotes themselves looked like this:

"Mentioned by Naisbitt and Aburdene in Megatrends for Women, page 56; Drucker in Post Capitalist Society, page 73; Sargeant in Androgynous Manager, page 16; Toffler in Powershift, page 145; Gardner in Building Community, page 7; Newsweek article......."

I figured that by the time the book was done, it would have 450 pages of reading, one third of which would be footnotes!

So, much to the consternation of one English teacher and two Ph.D.s I spoke with, I decided not to try for the Pulitzer Prize for research and instead, make the book as user-friendly as possible by listing all the references I used in a Bibliography at the end of the work.

Where I was leaning heavily on one or two sources for any particular section, I shared that in the text so that readers could have specific references to look to for more on the topic.

By the time I finished the book, a year after its beginning, it was clear that a few works in particular became almost constant references for what I wrote.

Those are:

1. John Gardner's *Building Community*.

2. Alvin Toffler's *Powershift*.

3. Joel Arthur Barker's *Future Edge*.

4. John Naisbitt and Patricia Aburdene's *Megatrends 2000* and Naisbitt's original *Megatrends*.

5. Faith Popcorn's *Popcorn Report*.

6. Larry Kennedy's *Quality Management in the Nonprofit World*.

7. Stephen Covey's *Principle-Centered Leadership*.

8. Peter Drucker's *Post Capitalist Society* and *The New Realities*.

I will also admit that two other little books helped a lot when my deadlines became too short or the writing began to take over my whole life, leaving almost no time for anything else. Those gems and gentle reminders to keep things in balance and take a deep breath, were Benjamin Hoff's *The Tao of Pooh* and *The Te of Piglet*.

Wisdom does indeed come from unexpected sources, footnotes or no footnotes!

Sue Vineyard, August 1993

INTRODUCTION

In his book, *Post Capitalist Society*, Peter Drucker tells us that:

> *"Every few hundred years in Western Society , there occurs a sharp transformation...(where) within a few short decades, society rearranges itself...its world view; its basic values; its social and political structures; its arts; its key institutions."*

When such a shift happens, he notes, people who are only involved with the new transformation cannot even imagine how it looked before.

Such is the case with volunteerism today as it emerges into a new maturity...a maturity which is vastly different from older patterns of 20 and 30 and 90 years ago.

The cartoons I've drawn in my trainings of "Polly do-Gooder" and "Volunteerus-Exhaustus", showing stereotypical volunteers of old.....white, female, rich, compliant, mother of two not working outside the home ....is so foreign to many modern volunteers that it is beyond their imagination.

The transformation is to a modern American volunteer who is more typically working one or more jobs, juggling career and family, is starved for time, living with stress, and thinks carefully before selecting any volunteer assignments; a volunteer that is as likely to be male as female, non-white as white, poor as wealthy or single as married.

This transformation comes in the wake of a global shift, or new paradigm, that is evidenced by the fall of Communism, the disintegration of the Soviet Union, the rise of Japan as an economic power, the emergence of the Pacific Rim countries, and in America, the women's movement, computers, communication technology, space travel and "instant" everything!

Both my children, late Baby Boomers, cannot imagine a different world!

Drucker believes that the trigger to the transformation in America, was the GI Bill, which gave our World War II veterans the money to attend college, thus enlightening millions during a rather short span of time, and empowering them with knowledge and perspectives much broader than ever before.

This, coupled with significant changes in women's work patterns and roles, issued in The Knowledge Society, which will probably continue until 2010 or 2020.

Why am I telling you all this at the start of a book on volunteerism? Because it is one of the major megatrends that impacts what we do and a classic example of information we must have as we map our future.

Changes and characteristics of the larger society turn up again in the microcosms that are our programs and by noting them here we equip ourselves for their fallout in our daily work. It is to this end that I have written this book, which attempts to explore all of the major trends that frame our lives, to discover the impact they have on what we do.

Just as we see America shifting to a knowledge society, we must also shift as volunteer program executives to be information experts who are constantly on the lookout for new knowledge. We then must find ways to share it with those people who need it in order to make our visions come true.

VOLUNTEERISM SHIFTS

The impact of wider trends on what we do has been reflected in volunteerism's evolution through the years.

In the early days of the 20th century, workers did what they were told, were dutiful employees, and did not look for rewards beyond a paycheck or any satisfaction that they might personally experience for a job well done.

The pattern of volunteering mirrored this. In the early 1900's volunteers were told **where** to come to do **what** work (roll bandages etc.), were often recruited by guilt or sense of duty...especially as benevolence for the "under classes"...and were mirror images of workers in our society who did as they were ordered.

There were exceptions, of course. The union movement, women's right to vote, child labor laws, are all examples, but for the most part volunteers were a compliant band of workers who did their work with as little notice as possible.

From the 1940's, when the management revolution began to dominate the American workforce, our Polly Do-Gooder became the norm, offering a stronger profile than before but doing assigned work with little questioning, rarely seeing, but always being in, a specific box on some directors management chart.

In the 1960's and 70's volunteerism began to emerge as a third sector (called an Independent Sector by Peter Drucker) in our society, along with the traditional Public and Private Sectors.

Though considered a weak cousin at first, our sector created leaders and visionaries such as Harriet Naylor, Ivan Scheier, and Marlene Wilson who offered new perspectives for the world to view us and us to view ourselves.

.....Hat Naylor brought her social-work ideology to volunteerism and argued in her 1967 book, *Volunteers Today: Finding, Training and Working With Them,* that those who work with citizen volunteers need to know more about them and how to work with them:

> *"This book pleads for consideration of volunteers as persons. It describes some conditions which would increase their effectiveness and the satisfaction they and others receive because of their service..... volunteers are made or broken by the practices of executives, program and service staff, volunteer offices, etc. etc."*

Throughout her life as author, teacher, advocate, and mentor, she addressed the issues related to how it **feels** to be a volunteer, and how those feelings become a critical ingredient for good working relationships between volunteers and the people who direct their efforts.

In her introduction she stated:

> *"This book expresses the need of each volunteer to be treated as unique and valuable, to become involved in the lives of others, to be awed by difference and enjoy building unity out of diversity."*

Along with Harriet Naylor's work, Ivan Scheier, Ph.D., in the early 1960's, added his voice to Hat's message, and called on our sector to recognize its diversity along with its commonalties.

As founder of NICOV......the National Information Center on Volunteerism, first formed strictly for those in criminal justice and later expanded to all varieties of our sector....he began to share his vision of a wide variety of volunteer efforts well beyond those that are institutionally based.

An advocate for the power of grass-roots volunteer efforts, he championed his conviction that the strength of volunteering comes when people collaborate, sharing information, gifts and needs.

He was based in Boulder, Colorado, and gathered around him a small group of people he felt might be interested in creating a structure through which citizens could be linked to programs in need of their assistance.

Among that group was a young lady who was indeed interested in this concept and volunteered to be the first part time director of the fledgling Volunteer Information Center of Boulder. That young lady was Marlene Wilson, who, during her tenure there, and with the guidance of Ivan and others from the area, turned the VIC into a dynamic force for volunteerism in the community.

Marlene's 1976 book, *The Effective Management of Volunteer Programs*, offered a clear translation of the principles of management to the volunteer sector. It also coincided with the growing reputation of the week-long Volunteer Management Program Ivan and she introduced at the University of Colorado in Boulder in 1972.

As we enter into the new transformed society at the end of one century and the beginning of another, our field builds on the contributions of these leaders and others who stretched our horizons and strengthened the numerous efforts of voluntary service.

This book is based on my belief that we live in a new, dynamic and transforming society that demands an updated approach to our work, our institutions, our co-workers, consumers, and society at large.

Just as there has been a change from belief in salvation by society to an emerging one that values individual responsibility, self-renewal, spiritual growth, capacity building, ethics and creative collaborations, there is also a need for change in how we chart effective routes toward our missions.

Each of us will have to map our own path to what we define as success. There cannot be a single route or formula. There is no guaranteed, one-true-path toward realization of our dreams, but a variety of options to be used and laid aside as circumstances, people and goals change.

In this knowledge age, volunteer program executives will have to know how to absorb information around them and extrapolate that which is useful, crafting it in creative ways to devise systems that empower people to reach desired results.

The trends and megatrends that frame our society and our existence within it, are critical for us to recognize and measure against the on-going question of relevance to work assignments. We constantly must draw from the massive information bombarding us, those critical pieces that can be fashioned into tools of action to help us achieve our dreams.

At warp-speed we are challenged to become part of societies great transformation, not simply as "tag-alongs" or "spectators", but as part of the driving force of participants who envision a brighter tomorrow and are practical enough to understand that it must be built on a better today.

Megatrends & Volunteerism helps sort through the massive information available and shares it with you in editorial fashion which you can embrace or reject. The Bibliography at the end of the book lists the sources I read and incorporated somewhere it these pages. It will be up to you to sort through the list to find those works that have the most bearing on the challenges that face you every day.

If you are one of the 1 in 100 readers who devour this entire book at one sitting, you may begin to question why I repeat discussion of certain trends in different chapters.

This is not an editorial oversight, but a realization that megatrends impact us from many angles simultaneously. Tribalism, accountability, the age of information, individualism, time & safety concerns and the call for relational management and shared leadership, for example, are driving forces behind most of volunteerism's new directions.

They therefore appear in several chapters, from slightly different angles, and are discussed so that the 99 out of 100 people who read this a chapter at a time or only selective ones, understand their impact.

The road to the future is as short as tomorrow and as long as 'forever'. It is more easily traveled when a good map is at hand, and I personally believe that good maps are formed by compiling solid information, clear directions and offering the signs that tell you what's ahead.

Enjoy the journey.

> *"Success is the quality of the journey."*
> ......Jennifer James.

Chapter 1

VOLUNTEER COMMUNITY AND NATIONAL SERVICE

"A debt of service is due from every man to his country proportioned to the bounties which nature and fortune have measured to him."

...Thomas Jefferson

"If you really want to be the best citizen of your country, you have to give something back to your country. National Service will mark the start of a new era for America where every citizen can become an agent of change and ready to transform the world in which we live, city by city, community by community, block by block."

...President Bill Clinton 5/30/93

As we look toward a new century, we will see organized community services take shape that will remind older people of the 1930's Civilian Conservation Corps (CCC) and younger ones of the Peace Corps.

At the federal, state and community levels, groups of workers willing to give service for the common good, are picking up their banners and marching to the drumbeat of those in need of shelter, health care, food, support, culture, education, transportation, a safe environment, mentoring and other causes serving society.

In the early days, the focus is on services for youth, including an emphasis on higher education credits. Soon the focus will expand to include people of all ages, offering the entire spectrum of

9

American society numerous opportunities to give back to our rich land a measure of service to benefit everyone.

Before we get to a full expansion of national service, however, we'll have to detour occasionally as we argue about wording, philosophy and definitions....a waste of energy if it goes on too long; a waste of people if it excludes any of the diverse pockets of our population willing and able to help make our country even richer in it's depth of compassion and concern.

YOU SAY 'TOMATO' AND I SAY "TOMAHTOE"......

A good friend of mine recently completed the final draft of a manual for a large national organization deeply involved in volunteerism.

The piece, which detailed step-by-step plans for a voluntary youth program, was returned to her with the following comment:

> _"Your work is excellent and the process you detail is superb, but we must ask you to edit your work to remove any form of the word 'volunteer' and instead substitute the politically correct phrase 'community service'. The latter is the more accurate and we believe it will have greater acceptance with future administrations in D.C."_

Though my friend protested such a waste of time, energy and money, she met a stone wall of resistance and therefore proceeded to edit her work accordingly.

Far fetched? Sadly, no.....

When she turned to me to question such a mandate, I unfortunately had to share that I'd heard several cases where people in authority had decided that "community service" wording was in and "volunteer" wording was out.

The entire discussion of the trend of volunteer community and national service (my compromise phrase) must begin with a plea for inclusionary language rather than exclusionary. Trying to erase the word "volunteer" and substitute "community service" is a fruitless effort born of a misguided belief that the concept of voluntary action must be popularized periodically to make it acceptable. An attempt in the 1970s to move away from the word 'volunteer' to 'citizen participation' and 'citizen involvement' demonstrates this classically, as those phrases are rarely used today.

Volunteerism is not a product requiring new packaging in order to sell it.

It is a concept as old as the earth and ingrained in Americans as none other save patriotism...which in many cases, are interchangeable ideas.

Do not misinterpret what I say as a rejection of the phrase "community service". I believe there is room for both phrases and several others within the scope of the definition of giving oneself in service.

My original art-teacher training rises to the surface when I attempt to help people accept the compatibility of both phrases and I find myself drawing the following to visualize them together:

Volunteerism is the fuel...community service is the vehicle.

Using the same analogy, we also can talk about the many diverse vehicles that can be fueled by volunteerism, and I'll do just that in discussing the megatrend I see regarding diversity within the ranks of volunteering in a later chapter.

The only points I'd like to make here are that we have, collectively, so many challenges before us of serving people, causes, and the future, that we do not have the luxury of time, energy or money to divert to senseless efforts of arguing about words or making anyone feel excluded.

> "What is it you do Mabel?"
> _"I'm a part-time senior-service, uncompensated community-service literacy-mentor program worker."_
> "Does that mean you are a volunteer?"
> _"I think so, but don't say anything. I have been sworn not to use that word."_
> "My lips are sealed."

So saying, let me address the issue of volunteer community service which is a major trend that will have new strength and meaning as we enter the next century. While exploring the topic, we might be well served to keep in mind a truism offered by major trend-watcher, Faith Popcorn:

"We're all in the future together."

MAJOR TRENDS THAT SET THE STAGE

In her book, _The Popcorn Report_, and in related writings from her organization, Brain Reserve, Faith Popcorn speaks of several major trends that are shaping our nation's habits, including the community service movement.

"Cashing Out" is how she labels the emergence of the quality of life as a top priority and the willingness to take less money and jump off the 'fast track' in order to have a better life.

That better life is defined as spending more time with family and friends, instilling values in our children and contributing to the general welfare of our communities. The trend has sent people into houses of worship in record numbers; seen corporate executives resign to move to a rural area to start an organic-garden business, and form cooperatives with other families to share work and live away from the congestion of cities, etc. etc.

Volunteer Community & National Service

Within this framework comes a mindset of community service, structured and spontaneous, which has both short and long-term benefits that can be felt and measured.

It may also prompt workers who took jobs fresh out of college based on higher salary alone, to explore new options of service where stipends and the promise of post-service credits may enable a career change to a suppressed desire to teach or work with the environment.

In what has been called by many the 'age of the individual', we may begin to see this major trend of 'cashing out' interwoven into the fabric of community service as people turn toward choices that allow them to put their values and desire for a better quality of life into practice.

Popcorn also reports on a trend toward 'time out', where people take a year or more off to follow other pursuits. This trend may provide new volunteers to tackle specific problems or share expertise with agencies working on issues they care about.

A third major trend reported by Popcorn along with John Naisbitt & Patricia Aburdene in their *Megatrends* series and Peter Drucker in *Post Capitalist Society* and *The New Realities.*, is the 'Save Our Society' thinking.

Basically all these authors are reflecting on a feeling among Americans that something must be done about the mess we're in, especially in the areas of education, ethics and ecology.

As the 'Save Our Society' attitude grows, the belief that community service—all of us working together for the common good, is also growing. This sets the stage for a variety of forms of volunteerism, created to address society's needs.

It must be abundantly clear to anyone examining the major trends of this decade, that the timing is again right for effective community action initiatives. We are a nation rooted in the value of volunteerism, and in times of stress such as today, we re-discover our need for community action and proceed to put it at the top of our agenda.

The challenge now is to identify existing programs which are already effective and replicate them, only designing new ones when older ones are not available or appropriate.

A NEW "SOCIAL COMPACT OF RESPONSIBILITY"

In President Clinton's inaugural address, he called on the youth and the young in spirit to give something back to their country, thus signaling his emphasis on community and national service for all Americans.

I label this initiative our new Social Compact of Responsibility, reminding us all of our history for service which was first formalized by the Social Compact of the Massachusetts Bay Colony in 1620. It also called all citizens to bear responsibility for the needs of people and common causes in their community.

First efforts in todays initiatives have seen the greatest emphasis on involving youth in service, drawing on existing programs such as Boston's 'City Year' program for direction and initial success. In later waves of activity, the scope of the participants will be expanded because of several undeniable trends and patterns:

1. **The population is aging.** This has two major impacts on community service:

   ☞ We will see needs increase for support in health care, housing, advisory, ombudsman, financial and recreation issues.

   ☞ We will experience a larger pool of potential volunteers ready, willing and able to serve community needs along side a shrinking teen population. We will especially enjoy more career-women entering the ranks of the retired who come with a broad expanse of skills, experiences and vital creative energy. After all, if Mom has been juggling career, family, friends and volunteerism for 45 years, why should we expect her to retreat to a rocker on her 65th birthday? Watch out world, here comes the true Auntie Mame generation!

2. **The average age of people taking college courses has inched**

up and up during the last several decades. A report on CBS news two years ago reported that by the turn of the century, 50% of those enrolled in college would be older than the traditional 18-24 years. This means that offering post-service credit for higher learning will not just attract youngsters, but people of all ages willing to exchange a year of community service for later educational opportunities.

Post service credit may even come in a variety of forms beyond college tuition credit, to include 1st home mortgages, tuition vouchers for job training, and possibly even small business start-up loans. Living stipends may be offered to enable adults to volunteer.

Adult placements may be closely tied to the service-learning concept where participants serve in the sites that also allow them to build skills. Placements such as:

1. Day care centers to enhance parenting/care-giving skills.
2. Community projects to strengthen organizational skills;
3. Conservation efforts to build skills of self-sufficiency (agricultural, home repair, etc.) and increased sensitivity to the environment.
4. Health clinics to enhance understanding of wellness.
5. Projects that can offer on-the-job training and experience in office skills, computer, communication, service delivery, human relations, etc. etc.

3. **There has been a loud cry to use existing programs** and not re-invent the wheel. In response to this demand, and coupled with an aging population, several efforts have emerged, including:

☞ Re-energizing and supporting existing ACTION programs such as Foster Grandparents, VISTA, RSVP, etc. and assisting national groups such as AARP, 4H and Extension,Scouts, etc. that tap adults for service positions.

☞ A merger between ACTION and the Commission for National & Community Service into the Corporation for National Service and the National Service Trust was proposed and also came with specific suggestions to NOT create an entire new bureaucracy, but instead to build on existing programs when possible.

As the new social responsibility efforts first take shape, many will despair, believing that all national efforts will be aimed only at youth. Time, however, will show that efforts to involve people of all ages will weave themselves into the fabric known as national service.

THE BROAD VISION

The Commission on National & Community Service issued a 130 page document, *What You Can Do For Your Country* in its first report to the President and Congress in 1993. It laid down the vision of developing national service built on existing state and local networks. Among the Commission's major recommendations:

☞ National Service need not and should not create a massive federal bureaucracy.

☞ National Service should be much more than a device for paying for college.

☞ Service efforts should be strengthened, especially in the educational arena.

☞ Participants should provide needed services not otherwise provided, so they would not displace employed workers.

☞ The federal government should only fund a portion of each program, while the rest would come from a combination of state, local and private sources.

☞ Local programs should compete for volunteers and funds. Competition among local service organizations would stimulate the rate of program innovation and improvement, while the best programs grow and the weak improve or disappear.

☞ Participation in national service should be voluntary rather than mandatory.

Catherine Milton, Executive Director of the Commission expressed the belief that in building a national service network, the focus should be on expanding the grassroots framework for service. *"What we need now is for the government to take a leadership role in generating a national sense of mission to fill that framework."*

In the midst of the focus on national service programs, my only caution would be that groups at the local level should not be so focused on federally supported volunteers that those people not interested in such government incentives, are pushed to the background.

I think this all may be labeled a "dangerous opportunity"!

NATIONAL MODELS

In selecting national models to lead off its efforts, a vision of service at the grassroots level was used as a blue print and in one case in particular, demonstrated an interest in service workers of all ages.

The Community Service Act of 1990 authorized seven model programs to test what might work best in facilitating a national service effort. One of the seven models funded in 1992, was the Delta Service Corps (DSC.) The DSC set as its goal the recruitment, training, placement and evaluation of 1000 workers, ages 17 and up, to work in pre-selected service sites in the counties and parishes bordering the Mississippi River in Arkansas, Mississippi and Louisiana.

Full and part-time participants were to be brought into the program over a three year period to positively impact communities in need of volunteers. They were offered a stipend during their one year contract and post service benefits of education vouchers for colleges within their states, or, for part-timers, vouchers for mortgages. Participants also received uniforms, health insurance coverage, training at basic, intermediate and advanced levels of service, project planning, communication and leadership in addition to skill building at the site.

Service sites were solicited through the media. They submitted applications that detailed their site, needs, available support and request for individual workers. Typically they offered positions in literacy, health care, child care, truancy or educational programs.

In the first year participants ranged in age from 17 to 82 with minorities actually being the majority. One worker in his 50's became part of the DSC in order to serve his community educational needs and to fulfill the dream of his grandmother to see one of her children go on to college. . .after his successful completion of his year with the corps, he planned to become a college freshman! Another participant intertwined his work on his doctoral thesis by establishing a youth program for a small community police department; a 53 year old teacher retired from her classroom in order to return to her parents county to help establish a literacy program.

The Delta Service Corps tests the viability of people placed as individuals in service opportunity sites. A second model program in Georgia, the 'Peach Corps'., tests the concept of teams of volunteers serving at sites.

Evaluations of the seven models under the Commission for National & Community service will offer clues as to how on-going national service efforts can be designed and implemented.

A NATIONAL YOUTH CORPS

In the efforts that concentrate on youth, there will be an on-going debate regarding philosophy until everyone involved recognizes that the diverse perspectives can merge positively into the overall goal of Youth Corps efforts.

There are basically three different views of 'youth service':

1. *Youth Development:* This perspective believes that the end goal of youth service is the development of the youth themselves who are exposed to service and volunteerism and benefit from involvement. Advocates see such efforts as positive steps to put

youth on the "right path", diverting them from negative influences, experiences and environments.

The services they perform, though important, are simply vehicles to bring the youth together, work together and be around others who can influence them positively.

Leaders of such efforts are typically answerable to their organization, which negotiates contracts with sites for service opportunities.

2. **Service-Learning**: This perspective believes that for the youth to truly learn from their service experience, the service itself must be meaningful and successful.

Proponents express belief that the service and the youth are equally important. Leaders are typically accountable to a school system, youth organization or church <u>and</u> the service site equally.

3. **Client-Oriented:** To confuse the issue even more, there is a third perspective that says the service is the primary goal and who delivers it or how they feel about it is secondary. Those in this category typically run community projects and are accountable to those projects and the clients they serve.

Although the definitions I offer here are extreme, it can help volunteer program executives to understand different perspectives when trying to work with groups that offer youthful volunteers.

NATIONAL SERVICE CORPS

Much in the pattern of the Civilian Conservation Corps (CCC) of the 1930s, a National Service Corps will be created and minimally funded through the national government. Additional money will come from community support and private funding.

It will be empowered and brought to fruition under the watchful gaze of the Presidential Office of National Service (ONS) with management and support through the Corporation for National Service and the National Service Trust.

Such a National Service Corps will address multiple needs and be modeled after the Peace Corps of the Kennedy era, offering community placement in pre-selected sites which have demonstrated specific need and the ability to support corps workers. Participants will receive allowances for living and post service credit. They will sign contracts for stipulated time periods of 1 to 2 years and work full or part time, singly or in small groups.

They will wear identifiable clothing so that the flavor of a uniform will be present and highly visible to the community.

Accountability, training and supervision will be important issues to insure the success of the workers and will also prove to be far more complex and difficult for Corps leadership than anticipated.

As leadership seeks to fashion the Corps, it will find itself appreciating the role of the professional volunteer coordinator more than ever before and eventually turn to seasoned veterans in the field for advice, leadership and direction. This will come after many months of trying to cope with the enormity of recruiting, matching, placing and managing Corps workers with little insight into the dangerous opportunities such a challenge represents.

Initial efforts will tag onto pre-existing programs such as Boston's City Corps and the Peach Corps in Georgia and offer great results because of the experience of their leaders.

The real test will come as the Corps ventures into new areas, trying to develop and implement systems for recruiting, screening, selecting and placing trained workers in a variety of sites.

Leaders active in the national service movement will divide fairly quickly into two categories:

☞ Those who believe the challenge is to recruit workers, and

☞ Those who understand that the real challenge comes after workers are recruited.

SUCCESS IS NOT GETTING SOMEONE ON BOARD;
SUCCESS IS KEEPING THEM ON BOARD IN FULFILLING
& EFFECTIVE SERVICE.

Volunteer Community & National Service

Corps leaders will encounter stumbling blocks as they attempt to work with and through existing systems that frustrate their efforts. For example:

1. If money must be passed through states, some will find a frustrating variety of rules and regulations for the disbursement of funds to workers, contractors and suppliers such as bid system requirements, etc.

2. Attempts to work through University systems will run into complex processes that must justify efforts and require massive paperwork and credentialling.

3. Plans to work with local town councils, municipal offices and organizations may need to endure endless hearings, committees and suspicions to determine control and authority, accountability and financial support.

All in all, the effort to bring the dream of a National Service Corps to fruition will be tedious and complex, but ultimately it will become a reality as it taps experienced programmatic and skill-specific leaders from the ranks of volunteer administration.

By the turn of the century, I believe the Corps will be a strong part of America's landscape, run effectively from the local levels with support from a national office. For true success leaders will have been careful to mold it in such a way as to stand the test of change in the White House.

Local communities and states will have been wise enough to create an organizational format that avoids the pitfalls of too much red tape, committee decision-making and bureaucratic babble.

My hope is that the Corps will, by 2000, become as much a role model and mentor to local community action as it is a direct service provider. Further, to be successful, it must be perceived as a funnel for workers to come through and which provides training and support and frequently, experiential learning equal in value to subsequent classroom education.

Its greatest potential contribution, however, will be three-fold:

☞ Establishing workers' commitment to a philosophy of life-long service.

☞ Providing direct service to alleviate the ills of society.

☞ Enabling further education and support.

Attracted at first to involvement for personal gain, Corps members will quickly become deeply committed to a better life for themselves and others, and will see the Corps as a vehicle to help all of us arrive at a brighter future.

The work will be hard, the challenges many and the demands complex. Where at first some who flock to the Corps will be most concerned with how involvement can profit them, workers will quickly sort themselves out between those willing to accept the role of community servants and those unwilling to do so.

The former will remain with the Corps and gain a life-long benefit through learning; the latter will drop out with hard criticism of structure and supervision and a puzzlement regarding the value of volunteering.

In the 20th century, most authors of 'trend' books agree that the G.I.Bill, used by returning military of World War II to go on to college, did more to change and advance America than any other single thing, as it introduced thousands to new educational experiences.

The national service effort, especially as it prompts workers to obtain higher education and a philosophy of community service, may be seen by future observers as an equally dynamic force.

DANGER!...WORKERS COMING!!....

The most dangerous part of the placement of Corps workers will be in those situations when community sites are not prepared for or able to effectively absorb the workers. A training system is necessary to equip the site managers to incorporate Corps participants. They will need to address:

1. How corps workers are placed so that they do *NOT replace* paid workers or substitute for a paid worker slot that could be created. The Corps must not be seen as simply a source of cheap labor.

2. How workers will be *trained* in job-specific skills.

3. How workers will be evaluated and held accountable to both the work site or project and the Corps *simultaneously.*

4. What *expectations* are realistic for the worker and the Corps support.

5. How *unsatisfactory* work can be addressed and workers removed if need be.

6. How sites will *interact* with Corps leadership and systems..paper work, reports, etc.

GETTING READY FOR NATIONAL SERVICE

Whether or not you agree with all its nuances, national service in all its various shapes and sizes will be a part of our life for the foreseeable future.

The "call to service" has gone out and is being heard, by individuals, by groups, by suddenly-interested parties now eager to put together programs that can meet needs from grassroots to mountain-tops. Large efforts, small efforts, structured and non structured, institutionalized and spontaneous, permanent and temporary.

What all this boils down to is several new breeds of volunteers coming from programs of all shapes and sizes. They will join the ranks of service-learning efforts through the schools and churches along with assigned volunteers from courts, businesses & groups, post-service learning programs, stipended, full-time and part-timers, those looking for very specific assignments, etc. etc.

The first step we can take to prepare for this onslaught is to simply accept this new internal diversity and see it as an opportunity to bring many different types of volunteers into our work. It is also a time to think about some basic realities of this new influx of volunteers:

1. **No program will be able to say "yes" to everyone who wishes to serve them.** There will be people who are inappropriate by reason of desired assignment, match with clients, timing, experience or background. Once again volunteer coordinators will have to remind themselves that their mission is to serve the clients or consumers of their organization, not the needs of different individuals and groups with the mission of community placement.

2. **For some federal programs, the local organization will be asked to financially support assigned volunteers.** Not every group can or should do this. You will have to address the question of funding by examining carefully your by-laws, philosophy, budget and mission statement. It would be wise to initiate a discussion now with your board and administration on what policy they might have or devise to address this issue.

3. If the national initiative produces volunteers in the numbers it expects from now till the turn of the century, we who are already in the field of volunteerism, **must accept some responsibility for making those volunteers feel welcome and valuable.** We have what the two Chinese characters for the word "crisis" mean: *"dangerous opportunity"*, as younger people increase their interaction with the world of service.

   The latest _Gallup Poll on Giving and Volunteering_ from Independent Sector, clearly shows a direct correlation between adult community service and positive youthful experiences with volunteerism. It is in our best, long-term interest, to work to make the experience young volunteers have as meaningful as possible, whether they work directly for our programs or in related ones in the community.

4. **We must be careful to insure that volunteers who come to serve in our agencies are not treated any differently than others already there.** Do not lower standards or expectations for such workers....it is demeaning to their potential and a slap in the face of existing volunteers who have to meet more exacting standards.

24

5. **Make sure there is careful monitoring of assignments so that no current volunteer or paid worker is displaced** by a newly assigned volunteer. If you are in a large program where paid staff work directly with volunteers, make sure the staff understands that the legislation enacting national service initiatives forbids displacement of current volunteers.

6. Recognize that any volunteers coming out of a formalized national corps or those from assignment-based programs in schools **come to you already having one supervisor from the parent organization and that the site supervisor is a secondary "boss".** This may mean that the worker will be required to attend trainings, meetings etc. for that primary group, taking them away from assignments on your site.

   Prepare to get specific facts on when workers need to be away from your work site due to demands of their parent organization. Federal corps workers, for example, may have to attend a specific number of days in training provided by the parent group......thus, no matter how much you need them on your site on a given day, the demand of the parent group will take precedent. Rule of thumb: PLAN AHEAD!

7. **Insure clear understandings of the roles between the site supervisors and the parent organization supervisors.** How well the roles are understood and agreed on will have a great deal to do with the success or failure of the intertwined relationships.

In addition to the basic philosophy and understandings listed above here are some other things you can do to prepare for community service workers.

☞ _Get The Facts...._

Keep up on what's happening at the federal, state, county and local levels. Ask to be placed on the mailing lists of any groups who might offer volunteers. The National Service Trust, the President's Office of National Service, your state Office of Volunteer Services, Independent Sector, Points of Light Foundation, etc. are all sources of information as well as _Grapevine: Volunteerism's Newsletter_, a publication with yours truly as Founding Editor. Also contact the county and local offices of school superintendents to ask to be kept abreast of any school-based service learning projects and contact local colleges for the same type of information. Ask the local Council of Churches for like news, etc. etc.

Understand that some of the federal efforts may offer credit for home or business mortgages, forgiveness of college loans or credit toward higher education tuition. All of these promises could make for some very persistent and anxious folks coming close to demanding placement.....if and when this happens, keep in mind your agency mission is not to absorb every such person pleading for an assignment!

☞ *Support the National Initiatives.....*

Expand your horizons to understand that the federal and youth-related emphasis on community service serves everyone in volunteerism, directly or indirectly. The more support you can offer by writing letters to Senators, Members of Congress, the Office of National Service, the White House, national/state/local politicians and groups to register your encouragement of community service initiatives, the better we will all be.

Get creative! Support legislation and efforts by having constituents sign letters of encouragement; start a phone chain to call influential people around the country! Get neighborhood associations, school classes, churches and synagogues, clients, patrons, funders, etc. to express their support! The louder we speak the more the powers that be will hear our cry to strengthen our Independent Sector!

☞ *Inform Others......*

As you gather information.....share it with others in our field. Find ways to contact and share data with other volunteer coordinators in your area. Set up informal meetings of program leaders to talk about ways to creatively tap new resources of volunteers. Keep constituents informed and ask them to share information with you as it becomes available.

☞ *Survey Needs....*

If you are not already tapping into a federal or state effort of community service, begin now to survey or assess your own organization as to new ways to interject more volunteers. Involve current volunteers and staff in the process, so that they are not only informed of the potential influx of new varieties of volunteers but also can suggest ways to integrate them successfully.

Are there places where extra hands would be greatly appreciated? Are there places where current volunteers could be moved onto if they had new faces to do the job they hold now? Are there spots where new volunteers would be totally inappropriate? Are there ideas for new services that have been shelved because there were not enough volunteers to take on such a project, that now could be instituted?

☞ *Address Screening Issues.....*

Now, before a dozen new people looking for community service placements come knocking at your door, is the time to address the issue of how much screening is required before specific placements can be made. You might wish to make a grid of available assignments and rank their need for confidentiality, specific expertise, danger, etc. This should give you a starting point on deciding what screening might be needed.

Some assignments require minimal screening, others maximum. Decide which jobs fall into each category **now** and then set the policies and formats in place to be ready for future use.

☞ *Address Training & Orientation Needs....*

This is a variation on the same theme as screening. Decide now what training is needed for the jobs you might assign new recruits. Use this as part of your decision-making regarding whether or not you will accept a community service worker placement. Also assess any danger and whether or not you feel such volunteers might be able to work around it. An example would be the danger of bloodborne pathogens such as Hepatitis B and if you believe certain volunteers could be adequately trained to risk coming in contact with blood spills in emergency rooms of hospitals, on ambulance duty for volunteer fire departments, etc.

Assess the amount of training needed for each job assignment. If the volunteer will only be available to you for a semester or even a year of work, do you really want to invest 3 months of training? Yes or no, you need to think about this aspect.

UNDERSTAND WHAT COMMUNITY SERVICE IS NOT!

As important as it is to understand what community service is, it is even more important to understand what it is **NOT**.

It is **not** a quick solution to all your recruitment needs. It is **probably not** a long-term assignment beyond a year or a semester (though it may grow into that later if the volunteer takes your mission to her or his heart!). It is **not** free..it will cost time, energy, adjustment, and probably money and increased reporting.

In many cases we will experience changes in policies, procedures and instructions as the programs develop. Plan now to be flexible and think through what the limits of that flexibility must be to be true to your organization's mission and capabilities. If you have a volunteer job that MUST have a rigid time schedule, it would probably be wise to avoid assigning a federal corps member who will need to be absent 3 weeks out of the year for trainings by their parent group.

Community or Public Service, in all its various facets, is not inherently good or bad, perfect or imperfect; it will instead be what we make of it at the community level, shaped in part by how well we fit this new diversity of volunteers into our existing efforts and how well we prepare for their inclusion in our efforts.

> *"All of us, whether or not we are warriors, have a cubic centimeter of chance that pops out in front of our eyes from time to time.*
>
> *The difference between an average person and a warrior is that the warrior is aware of this, and one of their tasks is to be alert, deliberately waiting so that when their cubic centimeter pops out, they have the necessary speed, the prowess, to pick it up."*
>
> .....Carlos Castaneda

PUBLIC SERVICE

In addition to workers coming from such a nationally organized effort, volunteer program leaders will face another category of participants in what many refer to as "Workfare". This is defined as a program involving those people who have benefited from welfare support for approximately two years and are then mandated to do public service or get an independent job.

Many workers, mandated to do public assignments, will have the expectation that community programs are equipped and waiting for such people-power. Sadly, if the field of volunteer administration does not find its voice soon, those who have the authority to deliver past welfare recipients to public services may have the same, unrealistic expectation!

Surprisingly, there still remains a false belief that simply throwing more people at a problem solves it. Also, there are those who naively believe any volunteer program director would be grateful for a call saying that 50 volunteers are "available" to work with them next week. Any experienced administrator understands that the real work begins when new volunteers come through the front door and that proper matching, screening, training and orientation, supervision and evaluation are all part of successful volunteer utilization.

With new sources of volunteers and assigned community and public service workers in our future, it will be critical for program and organizational leaders to be clear about what they can and cannot absorb into their efforts.

NATIONAL SERVICE AND THE 'SOCIOQUAKE'

There are several major trends which surround us and will impact the national community service initiatives, including a formalized Corps. None stand out more clearly than the 'Socioquake' talked about in the Popcorn Report, which is defined as a transformation in how Americans think, act and react to specific issues in society.

For the concept of national service to be welcomed by the public, it will have to effectively address and alleviate some of these issues which Americans say are upper most in their minds:

1. **Safety:** through programs addressing crime and drug abuse prevention; upgrade of housing; escort services for elderly and vulnerable populations; latch-key kids, etc.

2. **Survival:** through efforts for health care, prevention and wellness; counseling programs; fitness, etc.

3. **Environment**: through programs for reforesting; clean air and water projects, etc.

4. **Education**: by addressing concerns for literacy; through skill building, mentoring, tutoring, job training, etc.

5. **Ethics and Values:** by supporting arts & cultural programs to positively influence values; initiating accountability efforts; "ethics audits", etc.

6. **Youth**: through programs that positively involve youth or give parents an opportunity to expose their children to strong role models. Watch for schools to be supported by parents and citizens when they initiate service-learning programs or efforts that can help youth experience sound values, good decision-making, stress reduction, conflict management, goal setting, etc.

7. **Economy**: by demonstrating that community service workers are able to provide support as demands increase and funds shrink; through specially trained workers able to augment, not replace, workers on overload.

CORPORATE SUPPORT

In a poll by INC. magazine in May of 1993, the editors tracked the attitude of business leaders regarding community service. They found that a strong majority of those polled believed that business should "give back to society" and make "social responsibility a part of (the) corporate mission".

Seventy six percent felt that business can't be separated from other forms of social interaction, and expressed a belief that social responsibility is good business.

Volunteer Community & National Service

In tracking what specific actions or programs their company undertakes which they consider to be socially responsible, business leaders listed: Contributions to charity (80%), environmentally friendly policies (46%), employee support (32%), community support (29%), education support (20%), general volunteerism (14%) and other (22%).

It was encouraging to note that, 68% said they would continue socially responsible practices even if they found out their efforts were cutting into profits.

In specific response to the question of whether or not they feel businesses will need to continue to reach out as federal social programs become a reality, 90% of them said they felt their level of social responsibility would increase or at least stay the same.

As one company executive stated, "There are too many problems that are growing exponentially. And the government can't possibly do it all. We need to fill the gaps in what the government can't afford to do."

This survey, along with the observations of many trend-watchers, offer us hope that the time is indeed right for a resurgence and broadening of community service.

As we focus in on our concerns and see volunteers from teens to centenarians willing to help resolve them, our spirits should lift as we enter an age of optimism, recognizing again that Americans with their backs to the wall typically rely on volunteerism to see them through rough times.

Though our definition of volunteerism will be stretched to, and sometimes beyond, the limit, we will recognize it as the spirit of compassionate resolve that has defined our country from times preceding even the Pilgrim's arrival.

The formalized National Community Service initiatives, including a variety of Corps, are simply additional vehicles in a long and varied line of efforts that bring together the needs of our land and the people willing to serve those needs.

**The 1990s and turn of the century
will be remembered as the Decade of Service.**

Megatrends & Volunteerism

Chapter 2

CULTURAL DIVERSITY WITHIN THE RANKS OF VOLUNTEERISM

"A lack of trust inhibits the flow of information, sharing of resources, and reciprocity of influence. It usually leads to deteriorating problem solving and lack of detection of appropriate and underlying problems."

Catherine Sweeney, Ph.D.
"Teamwork & Collaboration in Volunteer Groups"

"We must unite our people, not divide them. We are one, we Americans, and we must reject any intruder who seeks to divide us by race, gender, or class. We must honor cultural diversity. We must reject both white and black racism."

..........*Barbara Jordan*

A great deal of attention has been given recently to cultural diversity. Those who train on the topic have their phones ringing constantly as clients seek to understand, attract and work successfully with culturally diverse people.

Before we can delve into an examination of diversity within the ranks of volunteerism, however, we must first step back and take a long hard look at what we mean when we use the phrase "cultural diversity".

Traditionally, the definition has been a narrow one, focusing on ethnic origin, race or nationality. With such a narrow perspective in mind, identification of "culturally different" people was limited to skin color, language or accent.

For us to truly take positive steps toward bringing a widening pool of volunteers to our programs and establishing long-term relationships with them, we must first redefine cultural diversity.

WE ARE ALL CULTURALLY DIVERSE

When our oldest son Bill was small he happened upon what for him was an incredible discovery.   At the end of his first day in 5 year old Sunday School, he came rushing out the door, eyes wide and excitedly taking Wes' and my hands to pull us back into his classroom to show us two new friends he had made.

"Look! Look, Mom and Dad.....they are two same-guys!"

What he had seen for the first time in his short life was, of course, identical twins. His vocabulary did not include the word twin, let alone the concept or biological understanding of how two little boys could look exactly alike. To Bill they were "the same" thus the term "same-guys" fit what was before his eyes.

And alike they were....size , shape, voice, actions, and enhanced by being dressed alike, these two confounded everyone but their parents, making it impossible to know if you were talking to Brad or Phil.

Several years ago, I ran into their mother while training in South Dakota and was brought up to date on how those wonderful "same-guys" were doing, as they had moved from our town many years before. She reported they were just fine and I noted as she spoke of each one individually, that they had developed very different interests and directions as they matured.

In thinking about the twins and the different turns their lives took, we stumble upon a basic truth about diversity: that no matter how much people may look or sound alike, they are different one from another; they are diverse, even if they start out in life as "same-guys"!

In examining cultural diversity, we need to have a very broad understanding of the term 'culture' which is defined by the American Heritage Dictionary as *"The arts, beliefs, customs, institutions, and all other products of human work and thoughts created by a people or a group at a particular time."*

With the exception of siblings, we all are born to different cultures by the nature of coming into a birth family that is unique to itself. Even siblings differ if that birth comes in different parts of the world. I, for example, was born into the Wylie culture and spent the first 6 years of my life in Davenport, IA with Mom at home, no brothers or sisters, and Dad on the road as a salesman who was gone from Monday through Friday as he worked his sales route for the Pet Milk Company.

My sister Jane, on the other hand, 7 1/2 years later, was born into the Wylie culture in Chicago with Mom at home, a big sister and a Dad home every night from the Pet Milk office in the loop. Already our customs and institutions had become different from one another.

Because we are shaped by the experiences and environments around us, we begin to carry around a wagon-load of 'diversities', defined by American Heritage as *"distinct in kind, unlike; having variety in form"*.

I therefore, before graduating from college and going into my adult life, was: Susan Kay Wylie, white, Methodist, female, first born to parents of Irish, German, Scottish and English origin, closely tied to extended family immersed in teaching, arts, music, innovation and societal contributions.

The example could be carried on and on through the never-you-mind years since I was 22, but the point is made that we all differ from one another and are therefore "culturally diverse", *"distinct in customs, beliefs, and structures"*.

When this understanding is internalized we begin to see that cultural diversity extends far beyond skin color, religion and ethnic or geographic origin. Hopefully, this awareness will help us respect our differences and blend our unlike backgrounds for common good, focusing not on what is different about us but what we have in common.

Now, here's a little test to show that we are gradually moving in that direction:

> Quick! List the religions & home states of the President's cabinet......

I'll bet you can't do it, yet just 30 short years ago, religion was such a focal point in elections that John F. Kennedy, a Catholic, had to deal with it directly, assuring people that he would, if elected President, **not** take his orders from Rome! He also was turned down by Senator Abe Ribicoff for the Attorney General's job because, as Ribicoff told JFK, _"it would not help the cause to have a Jewish attorney general putting Negro kids in schools in the South."_ (Boston Globe, 1993. Ellen Goodman, "Bean Counting Through the Ages).

Religion was an issue. So was geography, to the extent that at one time the Constitution wouldn't allow a president and vice president from the same state to serve together.

Now, because we feel religion and national geography are not relevant to how well a person can perform, they have become non-issues. (Although some may still need assurances from appointees that religious convictions will not hinder carrying out responsibilities. It is doubtful, for example, that a strong Christian Scientist would not have to address many questions if nominated for Surgeon General).

In another 30 years we may see other diversities becoming 'non-issues'.....race, gender, age, ethnicity, first language, educational level, physical abilities, etc. etc. because we have matured to the point of accepting as normal, the diversities among us and focus instead on what we can accomplish when we address mutual goals and concern together.

For the field of volunteerism, this new enlightenment is necessary for growth and survival, and it must come quickly as we examine ways to attract an expanded pool of volunteers and learn to embrace new definitions of "volunteers".

Individualism is a general trend that effects our efforts. Paradoxically it helps us all accept diversity as normal and causes us to focus on people as unique partners in shared goals.

EXPANDING OUR VOLUNTEER POOL

In its Volunteer 2000 Study , the American Red Cross listed 10 principles that must be present to support any successful volunteer effort. The first two address the issue of diversity:

☞ Defining who is a volunteer in an ethical yet **INCLUSIVE** manner.

☞ **REMOVING BARRIERS** to volunteering so as to broaden the potential volunteer pool.

In the American Red Cross study, they defined volunteerism as being:
- service to something beyond oneself;
- a contribution of time or effort outside a formal for-pay relationship;
- a contribution of time and effort beyond normal personal responsibilities.

In the decade before us we must be careful to draw our "boundaries" around volunteerism in such a way as to include all varieties of people who give of themselves for the benefit of people or causes they care about. We must reject any effort that excludes anyone because they are "different" or because thay do not fit a typical definition of a volunteer.

The needs of society and this little blue planet are too great for us to waste time debating who is a pure or capable volunteer and who is not.

Who can say that an adult with mental retardation or a quadrapelegic is not capable of an appropriate volunteer placement?

And who is to judge that a person assigned to your hospital by a corporation or classroom teacher and at first, reluctantly there, does not <u>become</u> a willing volunteer after experiencing the joy of serving others?

I don't know about you, but I'll decline the privilege of sitting in judgment on that!

In volunteer administration, you can bet your last recognition week poster that we will have to integrate into our systems a diversity never seen before if we are to expand our volunteer pool dramatically. This will include people who:
- are physically challenged.
- speak different languages than English.
- come from different ethnic and value backgrounds.
- are mandated by those who have control over them: teachers, ministers, bosses.
- are stipended and working with a national or state level corps.
- have little formal education.
- have very limited economic resources: money, phone, housing, transportation.
- have limited time or energy.
- are as young as pre-schoolers or as old as centenarians.
- have only very specific skills they wish to offer.
- live in remote areas.
- are home bound by physical limitations, safety concerns, family circumstances.
- are motivated by specific needs....resume building, relationships, debt repayment.
- are mandated by a group.
- need credit or experience.
- are out of work and looking for skill building or connections.
- wish to express their philosophy or values in tangible actions.
- wish to extend their service beyond a paid job.
- use the activity as a remediation of ills: self help groups, recovering addicts.
- have limited intellectual skills.
- are mandated or pressured by a need to get off welfare roles.

The list could go on and on, with endless categories of diversities and "cultures".

Our challenge in bringing a widening pool of volunteers to our efforts will come in identifying differences and any barriers those differences present to volunteering, then removing the barriers so that people who wish to serve can indeed do so, effectively and with dignity and appropriate recognition.

One of the most powerful trends of the coming years will not be how long our list becomes but how we find ways to integrate new people into the businesses we are about; how we work through our differences to address common concerns, needs and issues; how we come to a philosophy that says: "IF IT DOESN'T MATTER, DON'T LET IT MATTER."

"Who was that masked volunteer, anyway?"

Let's look again at the American Heritage definitions of 'culture' and 'diversity', and add the word 'voluntary' to our closer examination:

Voluntary: _"Not accidental; intentional. Arising from one's own free will. Normally controlled by individual volition. Acting by choice and without constraint or guarantee of reward."_

Culture: _"The arts, beliefs, customs, institutions, and all other products of human work and thoughts created by a people or a group at a particular time."_

Diverse: _"Distinct in kind, unlike; having variety in form."_

As we mature in our field, we are coming to accept and embrace 'cultural diversity' among the volunteers and staff whom we find in our programs. We will now need to extend this same acceptance within our own ranks, finding and embracing more and more varieties of people labeled 'volunteers'.

We now find a widening list of variations on the themes of volunteerism, volunteer and voluntary action. A beginning compendium reaching from one extreme to the other might include:

1. Volunteer, no tangible compensation whatsoever.
2. Volunteer, getting reimbursed for expenses.
3. Volunteer, on stipend.
4. Volunteer, getting credit for future redemption by their own choice.

39

5. Volunteer, getting credit immediately (school, etc.) by their own choice.
6. Volunteer, getting credit immediately or in future for redemption, as assigned.
7. Volunteer, doing work as part of a group; assignment by choice.
8. Volunteer, doing work as part of a group; assigned by others.
9. Person volunteering to gain experience, build skills or gain exposure.
10. Person assigned to work as volunteer for punitive redress.
11. Paid workers choosing to volunteer as a step toward retirement.
12. Paid worker assigned to volunteer as a step toward retirement.
13. Volunteer mandated to give X hours to retain membership in group.
14. Paid workers assigned to agency as volunteer by his/her choice.
15. Paid worker assigned to agency; no choice in assignment.
16. Paid worker volunteers to provide specific work skill in out-of-worksite placement.
17. Paid worker does volunteer work after hours at work site in different role than normal.
18. Paid workers doing more than assigned in his/her job by choice.
19. Paid worker doing more than assigned work because it's expected.

This is an overview, with many other definitions left out. We could argue as to how many truly are volunteers, but my point here is to simply caution us all that while the debate rages on, these folks will be at our door steps, offering help and expecting a warm welcome and hearty thank you for jobs well-done.

Let the debate rage on behind closed doors and within our family of volunteerism; let our door to the volunteers be opened wide so that when they come through it, they do feel valued. There is no more logic in raging at non-traditional volunteers about their "purity" than there is to rage at the airline counter clerk when a plane is late!

EXPANDING OUR INTERNAL DIVERSITY

At a recent AVA International Conference on Volunteerism, I had the opportunity to lead a discussion group for volunteer leaders involved in arts programs.

They voiced unanimous concern that they were perceived as second class citizens in the volunteer management profession and overlooked in discussions and plans for the future of volunteerism and community service.

They believed their "brand" of volunteerism was looked at as less important than human service volunteering, and that somehow, serving the cause of ballet or art ranked below serving Aids patients or adults learning to read.

I will now say the "unsayable" regarding the attitude some others in volunteerism have regarding them: *they are in many cases, correct.* A small minority of volunteer administrators unthinkingly do indeed rank arts as less important! (for shame.)

There are those who 'grade' volunteer efforts, with direct human service volunteer efforts in the "A" category, indirect human service volunteers getting a 'B', and those who serve the civic, environment, arts & culture, single issue causes and self-help groups somewhere in the 'C' or even 'D' ranks.

This is a form of score-keeping that pits oranges against apples and wheelbarrows against push carts. For us to grow and expand, it's a practice that has to stop.

As we step into the next century, volunteer administration will need to move toward accepting and actively engaging a widening diversity of volunteer efforts that might address:

Political Activism	In-kind Volunteering	Mentoring
Social Services	Athletics	Environment
Youth	Advocacy	Mobilization
Service Learning	Religion	Government Services
Arts & Culture	Media	Research
Foundation work	Fund Raising	Suicide

41

Megatrends & Volunteerism

Economy	Association work	Community needs
Safety	Prevention	Education
Military issues	Fraternal work	Preservation
Conservation	Health Care	Court assignments
Justice	Corporate efforts	

As we enter into a general trend that looks toward niches, we must resist the effort to only mingle with and involve like-niched folks from our particular brand of volunteering, but rather expand our inclusion to those who work with volunteers in varied efforts.

I urge every community to form what is commonly called DOVIA: Directors Of Volunteers In Agencies or DOVE, Directors of Volunteer Energy. DOVIAs usually are loosely structured support groups which gather periodically, have defined leadership and work to help associates gain skills, understanding and resources to be more effective whatever their niche.

DOVIAs traditionally value diversification and see themselves as stronger because of that diversity. They are self-help groups, information centers, support clans and resource treasure chests all rolled into one. Interestingly enough, they are NOT part of a larger, institutionalized organization and are therefore formed independently with individual differences geared to the needs of the group members....much like families who do whatever is needed and are ready to shift as needs change.

Fortunately, one leader in our field, Ivan Scheier, champions such groups and maintains a list of DOVIAs coast to coast, writing a bi-monthly newsletter called "Dovia Exchange" which is a regular feature within the GRAPEVINE newsletter for volunteerism. (see references)

When we address the issue of diversity, we must re-define it as an issue of **inclusion**, always widening our relationships to embrace the variety of volunteers that become available to us and the volunteer administrators and leaders who direct them.

When we learn to embrace those who differ from us in ways that must not count, we will come to be strengthened by the things we have in common and are, in reality, the only things that DO count!

DIVERSITY THROUGH AGING

One major shift we see nationally that will effect us dramatically, is the impact of diverse categories of our population by **age.....with particular attention to the youngest and oldest segments of our society.**

There will be an explosion of youth programs developed or highlighted by the turn of the century. Schools will involve students through service-learning projects in community-service classes where they will study the history of voluntary action in America and then adopt and carry out service projects.

Now is the time to contact grade, middle, high and vocational schools as well as junior college, and colleges/universities to influence how they instruct, direct and manage students. It would be disastrous if a dozen schools in a town decided to have students do 'public service' without involving those program administrators such as yourself, who would be responsible for integrating students into the community efforts.

Be sure to alert educators and church school leaders to the reality of your position should they plan to send students your way. Do not be offended to find people who lack real perspective of what it takes to involve, place, supervise and hold accountable, individuals or groups of volunteers.

Be especially careful to explain any screening that might be needed before you can accept volunteers. Share timelines for any necessary training and orientation and how students would be managed. Don't go into cardiac arrest if an educator insists that you must accept all student volunteers they send your way. Keep calm and explain that the rules of your organization must prevail when any volunteer, including their students, come to work for your agency.

A thorough, realistic presentation to teachers and leaders interested in student volunteer projects and service/learning efforts would probably be an excellent idea. At that time you can influence expectations on how students can serve in community programs.

Be sensitive (not defensive) to misconceptions some may have about volunteers. Correct any misperceptions with data and examples to re-direct thinking. Some common fallacies:

☞ Every organization offered students will be eternally grateful.

☞ Volunteers are simply free staff for groups.

☞ Volunteer directors can find somewhere to fit in every student.

☞ Volunteer programs that already have youth divisions will be able to handle last-minute or large numbers of new student volunteers.

☞ It really doesn't take much effort to manage volunteers. Simply getting a student a volunteer assignment, and thus exposure to service, is the goal. How well they do on the assignment is not really important.

☞ The volunteer administrator primarily becomes answerable to the providing institution which supplies students, rather than the agency accepting the volunteers.

☞ Student volunteers, once accepted into an agency program, cannot be fired.

☞ Any costs for supervising the students will be borne by the volunteer agency.

☞ The institution sending students can impose reporting requirements on the agency without prior negotiation.

☞ Past interaction between students and agencies insures future involvement.

☞ Students will only have to adhere to the sending institution's rules, not the accepting agency.

To avoid any horror stories later on, make expectations very clear BEFORE signing a contract. I believe this *has* to be contractual; a handshake is fine, but back it up with something in writing.

OLDER:

It can sometimes be difficult to think of age as creating diversity, but in fact, it is one way to categorize people. Just as we must be prepared to work with the distinct characteristics of youth and their institutions offering service learning volunteers, we must also be able to absorb effectively our growing number of aging citizens.

Less likely to come through an institution, these folks will come from smaller groupings, such as retirement and pre-retirement programs, families, church circles and neighborhoods as well as individually. Lesser numbers may be part of a variety of National Service initiatives or corps, established agencies in ACTION such as RSVP, Foster Grandparents etc. or may be part of school assignments as mid-life and mature people extend their life, health and vigor through continual learning and class work.

Prepare now for the unique characteristics older volunteers will bring with them to volunteer assignments. Draw on the wonderful seasoning and insight they offer and tailor work to meet special needs they might have.

OTHER DIVERSE CATEGORIES
COMING INTO THE VOLUNTEER POOL

This book is not intended to become a laundry list of varied diverse groups that might be part of volunteer programs in the next decade, but I do want to stimulate thinking about how current trends sketch out pockets of potential volunteers in new categories. For example, we will have opportunities to engage:

☞ Baby Boom women, labeled by John Naisbitt and Patricia Aburdene in "Megatrends for Women" as the *great archetype of the wisewoman*, freed up from family responsibility in later maturity and bringing to community service a great depth of knowledge and experience. Such women will gravitate to specific interests, and present distinct skills that can influence strategic planning, fund raising, board positions, investment, networking and a "can do" spirit for the whole organization.

Others in this 'culture' of mature, female ex-Baby Boomers may also respond to calls for volunteers to work on a particular project with hands-on opportunities. Watch for the 'counterpoint' effect in accepting assignments, those placements that require skills or activities **opposite** those they use in their jobs. (CPAs rejecting church treasurer jobs for work on the parsonage redecorating committee; teachers on the hospital grounds crew; lawyers baby sitting in the hospital nursery, etc.)

☞Women who are maturing and have become activists in regard to female health issues who may turn to health service and preventative care education agencies to volunteer. Keep in mind they will come with a great deal of background information and an agenda to meet needs in this specific arena.

☞ Couples and families who decide to volunteer with the dual agenda of spending time together while working on a service project. Parents may come in hope of influencing offspring on the value of helping others.

The Points of Light Foundations "Family Matters Project" offers examples and characteristics of families volunteering across America. These examples will increase as data shows more and more clearly the connection between youthful exposure to volunteering and volunteers and a positive value in adulthood for service and caring.

Bob and Nancy Gandrud and their children Janis, Jill and Jody have cared for foster babies for 15 years and have been named as a "spokesfamily" for the Family Matters program.

Bob, president and chief executive officer of Lutheran Brotherhood, and his wife Nancy speak movingly of their experience. "I started out looking into foster care as something I would do, but I quickly realized that it was a family affair. We

---

kept a schedule to make sure the babies were cared for -- with all of us taking turns at late-night feedings and diaper changing. We all learned a lot -- about life, about death, about choices and about each other," Nancy shared.

Caring for the foster babies helped the Gandrud family learn how to communicate with each other. "By the time I was five, we'd already talked about premarital sex," Janis said. "Those babies got us to talk about a lot of things -- sex, drugs, parenting. Having the babies and their mothers around taught us not to be judgmental of people. We learned to take responsibility. And we learned to negotiate to figure out who was going to feed the baby in the middle of the night."

Bob said, "I can speak from experience that family volunteerism draws families closer and makes them stronger. This helps families and their communities."

A 1991 Family Matters survey found that families are most often motivated to volunteer by the desire to pass community service values down to their children.

There will be several definitions of family to be considered:

☞ Step families: by 2010 one third of married couples will have a stepchild or adopted child .

☞ Single, female-headed households: in 1987 there were 2.6 million women who had never married and were raising children under age twenty one. 8.5 of 10 million single parents in 1990 were women.

☞ Unmarried couple households: 3 million in 1990, up 80% since 1980!

☞ Grandparent families: 3 million children lived with their grandparents, showing an increase during the 1980's of 40%.Other estimates place the number 3-4 times larger.

☞ Families formed by individual divorced parents sharing homes and responsibilities with others in the same boat, the 'Kate and Allie syndrome' if you will. Gay and Lesbian families: those with and without children.

☞ Families formed by maturing Americans banding together for mutual support by creating simple corporations or informal co-ops that buy or build a multiple-unit housing complex, share autos and vans, take advantage of bulk buying, shared equipment and resources plus services to one another in barter strategies.

☞ Families headed by bread-winning Mom at work and Dad at home with the care-giving duties of raising children and doing housework.

☞ Spiritual families bonded together by shared spirituality. Not just confined to religious ideology, they will expand to include issue of ecology, values, the arts, philosophy and shared visions of the future.

Diversity within volunteerism will be a major trend for the next two decades as we expand our volunteer resource pool and deepen our concepts of community or national service.

Internally, the ranks of volunteerism will swell by the inclusion of new forms and varieties of people who manage volunteer efforts and those already hard at work who were not traditionally seen as "part of the circle".

In that spirit, I believe we will accept new definitions of volunteerism, and though some debates will go on forever about "purity", our spectrum will broaden as we embrace a variety of definitions of service to others and experience new and innovative ways to remove barriers to that service.

In his book *Post Capitalist Society*, management marvel Peter Drucker talks about the trend toward "tribalism" and its underlying need by people to have a unique identity. He strongly states his feeling that the push to recognize diversity is simply a manifestation of this tribalism trend, and is actually a very divisive and negative movement.

48

Cultural Diversity within the Ranks of Volunteerism

Michael Eisner, CEO of the Disney Corporation has also voiced his concern over extreme demands of individualizing everything and cocooning to the point of no common ground. He points to the coming of 500 cable TV channels as a symptom of the death of any mass market or general public that intermixes a variety of characteristics in order to appeal to a variety of people.

I understand the concerns of both men, but actually see in these concerns an opportunity for volunteer jobs to be the meeting ground of different people who recognize their differences, but lay them aside to work on a common cause. Hopefully such merging will help us all realize that we are stronger _because_ of our diversity and the different strengths we can bring to assignments.

As volunteer program executives and leaders, it will be up to us to seek out and embrace different cultures and natural diversities among the volunteer workers, understanding that what makes us unique as individuals simply is a means of identification, to be used as a channel to connect people who are willing and able to help to those who need that help.

In summation, we will come to the point of maturation that allows us to focus not on what is different about us but what we have in common, so that together, we can bring the strengths of our diversities to bear on meeting the challenges we share.

**OUR DIFFERENCES WILL BE OUR STRENGTH;
OUR COMMON DENOMINATOR OUR SHARED VISIONS.**

Megatrends & Volunteerism

Chapter 3

GROWTH OF ENTREPRENEURIAL AND GRASSROOTS VOLUNTEERING

*"One thing I know: the only ones among you who
will be truly happy are those who have sought and found
how to serve."*

.....Albert Shweitzer

In the next two decades, volunteerism and community service will
see an explosion of new kinds of ventures that come from the
creative genius and entrepreneurial spirit of Americans of all ages.

THE VOLUNTEER AS ENTREPRENEUR

Peter Drucker, in "The New Realities", speaks about the Age of
Information bringing an explosion of entrepreneurship that is often
examined from the perspective of material civilization, goods,
services and businesses but rarely for its equally important impact
on social innovation.

*"Social innovations are equally entrepreneurial and
equally important... the present age of entrepreneurship
will be as important for its social innovations-and
especially for innovations in politics, government,
education and economics-as for any new technology or
material product."*

The volunteer as entrepreneur has already begun to make its mark on our land. Few better examples exist than Mothers Against Drunk Driving (MADD) formed by Candy Lightner after her daughter was run down by a drunk driver in California. Armed with a fierce passion and determination to get drunk drivers off the road, she banded together with other parents who had lost children to alcohol related accidents, formed MADD and ultimately changed drunk-driving laws around the country like no other group ever has.

Each day we hear of an individual, a set of parents or single-minded people who decide to do something about a particular problem and then set about doing it, ignoring all the naysayers who insist "it can't be done"!

Such efforts will become more and more prevalent as individuals take the initiative to remedy what they perceive to be a problem.

We will also see entrepreneurs who tire of complex beaurocracy surrounding an issue, starting up more simple efforts to get to solutions more quickly.

In one Illinois town a mother of a child with learning disabilities heard that the local park system offered a day camp in July for LD children. She inquired about the program and was given a packet to "complete and return". In it were instructions to provide the following:

1. Complete school records of the child with verification of the LD diagnosis.
2. Complete medical records and affidavit verifying LD status.
3. A statement from a licensed psychologist or therapist detailing observed behavior of the child after an individual interview session. . .minimum time: 1 hr.
4. Statements from the therapist and lead LD school teacher listing all activities the child should or should not participate in and why.
5. A full, current (30 days) medical exam report. potential side effects.
6. List of all medications taken by the child and a physicians statement per each of desired results, purpose and any potential side effects.

7. A parental release form to free the park system from any liability if the child is hurt.
8. A parent-signed statement acknowledging the fact that the child would not be permitted on the regular park bus, but must be hand delivered and picked up each day by parents.
9. A directive to come to the Park District office with a deposit of $50. _"If your child is accepted you will pay an additional $25 by check or money order within 48 hours of acceptance. If your child is rejected, you will get all but a $15 processing fee returned to you after 30 days."_

It was May when she got all this in the mail and as if not overwhelmed enough by the loops and hoops the list presented, the last item really brought down the house:

> _"Packet must be completed and returned to the Park Board no later than Feb. 1st. for consideration for the following July."_

Whee! Guess what she did?

Wrote "NEVER MIND" on the form, and sent it back to the Board.

She then went to a local private college and persuaded them to provide their site for one week in July plus 2 LD teachers-in-training and 2 Recreation studies interns to design a camp program for credit in class. She then went to the May meeting of the local LD parent group and asked for volunteers and suggestions for her plan of a one week camp experience; she sought and acquired funding from 10 individuals to underwrite the program and produced the form for parents to enroll their child in the camp.

Understandably, the form was brief:
1. List name, address, age of your child.
2. List capabilities and skills of child.
3. Sign here if you are willing to volunteer during the camp.
4. Send in $25 to address below.
5. What else should we know about your child that could help make this experience the best that is possible?
6. Suggestions:

53

As we come into the age of the individual we will find more and more people going off on their own to do what makes sense. Sometimes this will cause problems as they challenge established systems or as they overlook critical planning aspects, but for the most part, they will succeed ....because they are passionate, have a clear goal and don't know it can't be done!

As volunteer program executives become more sensitive to the entrepreneurial spirit, they will find ways within their system for such volunteers to satisfy their need to create and organize to accomplish a particular goal. Such harnessed energy will be welcomed and very valuable.

One rule of thumb such creative volunteers will use, even if they don't label it as such, is a philosophy of "Form Follows Function"; the form of the effort is not as important to them as that it be created to best respond to the need and facilitate the goal.

A Keep-It-Simple attitude will prevail because of the volunteers' need to conserve time and energy resources. The justification for creating something new will come from an accepted belief in taking responsibility. The processes of achieving the goal will be deeply influenced by the issues of time and energy constraints.

THE 'MISSED-OPPORTUNITY' VOLUNTEER

These are the people who have tried hard to volunteer for existing groups but never were able to do so. I am hearing more and more stories....and have a few of my own...of people who called a hot line number in response to a media advertising promotion asking for volunteers, only to get vague answers of where their help might be needed and a promise, soon broken, that "someone will get back to you".

It is not unusual to hear Chapter 2 of this story in the form of the disappointed potential volunteer 'giving up' on any existing organization and creating their own system to address a problem, or sadly, simply deciding to expend his or her energies elsewhere.

If we are going to use the media or other technological approaches to alerting the public to needs in the community, we must have a system that does not drop the ball at the time people respond to our pleas. I have cautioned many Volunteer Centers and individual groups who are ready to go all out in using the media to recruit volunteers, that they must have the systems and jobs in place and ready to go before they ask folks to sign on.

The people who benefit from our work cannot afford to let one potential volunteer slip away because there was no response vehicle to carry a willing volunteer to an assignment after being recruited to help.

Americans today clearly demand that the institutions around them be responsible and responsive. Thinking only about recruiting and failing to take the next planning step of how to place volunteers is just the opposite!

SOCIAL CAUSE ENTREPRENEURS

A variation on the theme of entrepreneurship will cause us once again to broaden our embrace of a diversity of people working for the betterment of others.

Though not classified as volunteers, we will have new partnerships with people who see a social need, clean air for example, and then form a company aimed at that cause. Such for-profit ventures will provide services or products that address the cause and assist in the necessary remediation of ills.

Privatization has already occurred in hospital and health care entities and been accepted by people as necessary to meet service demands. Those creative souls who design companies from the start because of a passion for a specific social cause will also be accepted.

SELF-HELP GROUPS

One of the best examples of entrepreneurship in America is the explosion of self-help groups to assist individuals and families cope with problems, addictions, fears and change in their lives. Name a concern and you can probably find a self-help group clustered around it. There is even a clearinghouse for information on locations of self-help groups around the country to assist people in finding support.

Many such groups are modeled on the 12 step program of Alcoholics Anonymous which leads participants through specific steps towards control and wellness. Others have adopted counseling steps, information only, self-revelation, confrontation and skill building to assist members.

Examples abound....*Tough Love*, to help parents cope with rebellious children; Ostomy groups helping members cope with colostomies and illiostomies; *Why Me?*, offering support to women who have had mastectomies; *Weight Watchers*, to assist with weight control (and sell products); Reentry groups to help those coming out of prisons or hospitals adjust to non-institutional living, etc.

In each of these cases, individuals dealing with specific challenges decided to gather others with similar problems to exchange information and support for adjustment and re-direction in their lives.

A variation of the self-help theme has been with us for years in the form of groups who recognize social problems and form support organizations to model or mentor those at risk. This reflects the deepening sense of responsibility people are feeling for the world around them and their understanding that what ills befall any part of our society, also befall all of us.

Examples include *Big Brothers/Big Sisters*, which match at risk children with adult volunteers in the hope of nurturing and influencing the children positively in formative years; *Parent Aide* groups made up of parents who are willing to become role models to parents deemed at risk of abuse or neglect of their own children, etc.

Another type of self-help group that began spontaneously because of shared concerns, are all the neighborhood watch and "Safe House" programs that identify a particular house in each block that children can run to if they feel threatened.

Newcomers Clubs have been around for decades and really represent a type of self-help group as they assist people who have just moved into a community to adjust, make new friends and learn about the area.

More and more churches and companies are providing the backdrop for self help groups for all manner of shared concerns: Newly divorced; laid off; new parents; parents of teens; widowed; people seeking jobs; singles; retired; step-families; people having financial difficulties; those living with life-threatening diseases or disabilities; families of recovering addicts; individuals working to make peace with abuses in their childhood; those facing major adjustments in their lives; bereavement, etc. etc.

All of these examples point back to the age of the individual acting as entrepreneurs who see a problem and then take the initiative and responsibility for doing something about it. It is grassroots volunteerism at it's classic best, the old barn raising spirit written in a new hand but drawing from the same 'can do' spirit Americans are known for.

ENTREPRENEURSHIP AND THE VOLUNTEER ADMINISTRATOR

When I first spoke about the trend toward entrepreneurship and grassroots entities, several volunteer coordinators confided that they thought that might mark the end of the professional hired to lead volunteer programs. Let me say that I do not believe this to be true at all...quite the opposite, I see emerging groups as potential employers of those trained professionals and a source of more people coming into our field.

Typically grassroots efforts fall into two categories:

First, those that address an ill, find a remedy and disband after solving the problem, and secondly, those that address an ill, find that the remedy is very complex or must be on-going and then grow into a formalized organization that requires more sophisticated leadership and management.

In the former case, the entrepreneur starting the effort is normally able to handle all that the effort demands with the help of several other supporters.

In the latter case, the healthier groups are led by a founder who recognizes any limits to their own ability to manage and lead and brings on those people who have the skills necessary to really accomplish the goal on a long term basis. Typically such a founder steps into a role of motivator, fund and friend raiser or guiding light, letting go of the day to day operations and remaining a powerful force to keep followers focused on the dream.

World Neighbors in Oklahoma City, an international aide organization that sends teams of experts into developing countries to provide agricultural, family planning, health care and leadership training, is a classic example of such a positive leader. Rev. John Peters and his wife founded *World Neighbors* around his dream of making a difference in the lives of desperately needy people world-wide. He lead its efforts with the support of many others who caught sight of the dream through Peters' vision, but then stepped aside to bring in necessary leadership to direct its increasingly complex challenges. His role remained until his death, as inspirational leader, drawing people to the organization and keeping the dream of the Good Samaritan as the center focus of efforts.

Sadly, there are far too many entrepreneur/founders who do not have the wisdom of Rev. Peters, and insist in keeping control of "their" organization beyond the limit of their own skills. It is typical that the founder is a visionary leader whose skills lie in persuasion, dream-catching, friend-raising and long-term thinking. What many groups need in their organizational development after their initial founding and growth, is a detail-oriented manager to take care of nuts and bolts, budgeting, reporting and organization.

If a founder does not recognize that these typically right and left-brained approaches can work together to further the dream and are complimentary, rather than competing, it is likely that the organization will experience a crisis and either die of self-inflicted wounds or split between competing leadership philosophies. Either scenario causes great pain and grief and ultimately, damages the cause the group was created to help.

Growth of Entrepreneurial and Grassroots Volunteering

Within the development process of grassroots groups, is an opportunity for the entrepreneur to recognize their lack of skills in volunteer administration, causing them to gravitate to our ranks, acquire training and become a skilled professional. For groups that recognize the need for skilled leadership and management, there are opportunities for the hiring of volunteer coordinators and administrative leaders.....thus expanding the number of job openings.

THE 3 R's: DRIVING ENTREPRENEURIAL EFFORTS

With a new awakening to the reality of our interconnectedness internationally, the paradox is that we also become aware of our interconnectedness at the most local of levels. We will come to understand that there is no "us" and "them", but a very broad "we" who must stand together to solve the ills of drugs, health care, safety, homelessness, security, natural resources, the environment, education, and on and on.

As I look over a dozen books and countless articles addressing trends, change and forecasts for our nation and the world, I see all of them fitting into three categories; the new "3 R's" for survival today and the future tomorrow:

RELATIONSHIPS   RESOURCES   RESPONSIBILITIES

Relationships: Having to do with how we interact, how we care about and for one another, how we relate to each other, ourselves and our surroundings.

☞ **Parents are concerned about their relationships with their children;** they want them to grow up to be happy, healthy adults who care about themselves and others; they work to model behavior and values so that their children can lead productive lives; they want to keep them away from gangs, drugs, guns, and negative influences.

☞ **Everyone is worried for their safety;** they believe that positive relationships of understanding and acceptance, the Rodney King philosophy of "Can't we just all get along?", must be brought into every home and neighborhood in the land. People are buying safety devices and security systems in record

59

numbers; too many handguns are too easy to come by, so folks stay in at night and close the drapes in public housing hoping that stray bullets do not invade their territory; taxi drivers have areas they refuse to service due to safety concerns; gays and lesbians watch out for skin-heads; the elderly fear muggings; and children fear daily life. Thinking people believe that developing better relationships will help solve the root problems that force such fear into the hearts of so many.

☞ **People are worried about their health;** too many are uninsured; some fear being dropped should a catastrophic illness generate more bills than an employer or insurance company will bear; Aids and Hepatitis B loom over the heads of everyone; we all hope for better relationships with government, insurance and drug companies so that we can work together to meet health care needs.

☞ **People are concerned with the environment** and how it affects themselves and their loved ones. Issues of clean air and water, soil conservation, forresting, wet lands, land fills, preservation, wildlife, open land and general conservation /ecology are increasingly on the minds of those who understand that our relationship with the earth and its diverse creatures is critical, not just to *their* future, but *ours* as well. Wellness will be defined in broadening terms through the next decade, encompassing the health and welfare of every living creature and the environment, and understanding that ecology extends to ourselves as well as others and to our earth.

Relationships are a basic driving force that will influence trends, actions and reactions for the years to come, and stimulate numerous entrepreneurial efforts.

Resources: Having to do with more than just money, but expanding to include an over-riding concern with Time and Energy and even Information.

☞ **People will continue to have to spread economic resources more thinly** as the economy slowly recovers from the age of spend, spend, spend. When the first economic pinch came after World War II, Dad got a part-time job...when it squeezed harder and greater demands were put on families for college, homes, cars and necessities, Mom went to work outside of the home....when the squeeze came to the choking level from outrageous increases in energy and health care and inflationary costs of goods, Dad got a second job or moved his family in with relatives while Mom struggled to hang on to her work while juggling family, children and aging parents. It will get better, but it will come slowly and probably never return to the Leave It To Beaver family patterns that were a reality in fewer homes than we might imagine.

 Time will become a resource that is spent as carefully as any dollars, and it will be a measuring stick for everyone contemplating involvement in any aspect of their life, including community service. Time with family, loved ones or individual interests will not only be desired but demanded and will drive decision making for the next several decades. 'Second-tier cities', (defined as those cities whose population and size allows people to avoid 1, 2 and 3 hour commutes to work) will allow parents the ability to go to their child's Little League game within 20 minutes of leaving the office or factory; cities that offer arts and culture, fun and amusement within easy reach and time frames, and community activities or service that allow people to spend precious time together.

 Energy will be considered a critical resource to be spent wisely and well. People are coming to realize that energy is not endless at any given point in a lifetime nor over the lengthening span of life. It is, therefore, to be rationed carefully...first to those efforts and people who mean the most to us, and then in widening circles of concern to other people and things. It will be spent on those efforts which return the most for the investment....returns of benefits, satisfactions, direct assistance or repayment of perceived indebtedness.

 In this, the Information Age, **knowledge will be seen more and more as a rich resource,** and our appreciation for gathering information will manifest itself in increased interest in education, life-long learning, developing of multiple skills, training and experiential learning. Service-learning opportunities will be highly prized at every level of education and adults and older youth alike will seek out and cultivate such opportunities. Information and knowledge will even become a bartering chip in relationships between people, corporations and nations!

Resource management will be a major concern for people for several decades to come, driving trends, actions and reactions across the nation, at both grassroots and wider national levels.

Responsibilities: The third major factor that will impact our lives is a growing awareness that we must take responsibility for our lives, our surroundings and our futures.

☞ _The Popcorn Report,_ the _Megatrend_ series, Drucker's works, and a dozen other leading publications, speak of the **'age of the individual'**. From "egonomics" to "niche marketing" to "vigilante consumerism" to "saving our society", we see these authors and others pointing to people becoming involved internally and externally as individuals, often banding together over common concerns to make a difference, take control and effect change. _Megatrends 2000_ calls it the _"1st principle of the New Age movement ..the doctrine of individual responsibility"_....an _"ethical philosophy that elevates the individual to the global level....recognizes that individual energy matters."_

☞ I expect to see a **revised welfare & entitlement system in America** that will demand that people take responsibility for their own life....to get a job independently or in public service programs after accepting welfare support for no more than 2 years if they are able-bodied; to pay child support as directed by the courts; to plan for their future and not see Social Security as the only source of income they will need in retirement; to avoid cheating the system and instill in those they influence to also avoid draining assistance programs unfairly.

☞ **People are taking greater responsibility for their own health** and seem to want to continue that trend into the future, so that they can have more control and well-being for the seven, eight or nine decades they will live. They also are taking responsibility for those around them...teaching children good health habits, sharing information that can prevent risks for pregnancy, Aids, substance abuse, etc...........designated drivers, parent-mentoring programs, health screenings, exercise programs, nutrition education & practice....all examples of taking responsibility for self and others.

☞ **Groups and agencies are taking greater responsibilities to insure that inappropriate behavior for vulnerable populations is prevented.**...screening of paid and non paid staff will become a more in-depth part of bringing anyone into work efforts and national and even international computers will allow us to check on backgrounds of workers quickly and inexpensively even in the midst of controversy over the right of privacy.

☞ **Responsibilities of government will shift from a Parent-to-Child model to one of a partnership.** We will move away from the Big Daddy mentality that says "Government's role is to take care of everyone" or that which believes "Government's role is to enable big business to prosper so it can take care of everyone" to a blended definition that sees government's role as enabling individuals and entities to work together, taking responsibility for themselves and their con-joined success.

Responsibility and new perceptions of its definition will be the third driving force to underline the trends, actions and reactions of the future.

From new awareness and concerns for relationships, resources and responsibilities, will come entrepreneurial efforts.

WELCOMING NEW PARTNERS

We live in the age of information and the decade of the individual. This lays the groundwork for people to play the role of entrepreneur, starting their own grassroots effort to address perceived concerns and needs for the greater good.

Megatrends & Volunteerism

Within the framework of this entrepreneurial spirit, volunteerism is shaped and defined by concern for resources, relationships and responsibility. It is the old barn raising spirit reshaped to address the ills of society and the hopes for a better future. It is the "can do" determination that first developed America through the efforts of native Americans and the Pilgrims who followed their lead.
The American Heritage Dictionary defines entrepreneur as " _a person who organizes, operates and assumes the risks of ventures_".

It is time for us to understand that more and more Americans will fit this definition in the years to come. It is up to our field to recognize the potential, enthusiasm and energy such people can bring to our efforts, either as part of our existing programs or as partners in community actions, and to find ways to work productively with them.

The spirit of American ingenuity and determination will prompt all manner of creative vehicles to address the challenges and concerns in our society.

Chapter 4

The Emergence of a National Leadership Group

"It is critical that the volunteer leader actually create a compelling vision that takes people to a new place and keeps that fire, by holding the vision in mind."

...Warren Bennis, "
Leaders: The Strategy for Taking Charge"

"Four overarching characteristics appear repeatedly in the best nonprofit organizations. These hallmarks (of excellence) reflect more than sound management practices, good staff and effective programs...although all are important components of excellence. But the very best groups consistently manifest something more...a clear and tangible value added."

.......Knauft, Berger & Gray,
"Profiles of Excellence: Studies of Effectiveness of Nonprofit Organizations"

By the turn of the century, I believe there will emerge a primary organization that will be hailed as the predominant leader-group to all facets of volunteerism. It will most likely come from one of the existing groups on the scene now, which has changed its form and public image to accommodate shifting needs in our growing sector.

It is clear from writings of such trend-watchers as Drucker, Popcorn, Covey, Aburdene and Naisbitt, that the need for such a group is already upon us. Americans everywhere seem to be searching for a central, trusted community that allows them to bring their strengths and needs to one meeting ground in order to learn from one another and share resources.

In the worlds of philanthropy and volunteering, Independent Sector under the leadership of Brian O'Connell, has provided such a community, but there is a growing demand for another, more programmatic leader-group, that can provide direct services in expanding volunteerism at the local level.

CLAN-GATHERER

Toward this end I would expect that a national group will emerge that will draw together specialty sub-groups which lead volunteer efforts in a wide variety of categories. Drucker's discussion of 'tribalism' in *Post-Capitalist Society* is one source that points the way to such a characteristic in this national group.

This national group will embrace and cultivate relationships with national and international groups, corps, foundations, and federal entities, to build working partnerships to empower and advance community service.

As the primary "clan-gatherer" it will act as a facilitator and bridge-builder among common concerns, bringing people together in a "neutral zone" that avoids territorial questions and helps everyone focus on what they have in common rather than where they differ or conflict.

This national group will provide a free-flow of information, help people link sharable resources, explore and provide program development assistance and evaluation, promote collaboration and coordination and generally facilitate working partnerships that avoid re-invention of the wheel, and appreciation for specialists joining forces to address challenges from a variety of perspectives.

The organization will command respect from all facets of the field, from the least to most sophisticated and institutionalized programs, because its' stance is positive, democratic and noncompetitive. It will not desire or attempt to control other groups, but support their differing efforts in a mutually beneficial and practical, win-win manner.

VOLUNTEERISM'S VOICE

Its leaders will be perceived nationally and internationally as a voice for the millions of Americans who call themselves "volunteers", although it will carefully not restrict it's constituency by only accepting the word "volunteer" as a title for those who serve. It will respect the cultural diversity within our ranks and welcome to its fold community and national service workers, interns, members, aides, organizational leaders, founders and workers from spontaneous, grassroots efforts, along with the hundreds of other titles people use in serving causes.

ADVOCACY AND RECOGNITION

This clan-gatherer group will have an advisory board which will actively advocate for the organization and its goals in Washington DC. The board will draw members and advisors from innovative voluntary groups, individuals and effective program managers. These people would be well-known leaders from the corporate, non-profit, business, political & voluntary fronts.

The group itself and its leadership would be a positive and strong force felt in state houses, corporate board rooms, organizational offices, political parties & programs, media & journalistic entities, the entertainment industry, union negotiations, pulpits and agencies of all kinds. Its clout would rival any advocacy group, as it is perceived to represent the majority of Americans, those who in any manner, volunteer.

RESPONSIVENESS

In response to the expressed desire of people to have customized attention (noted in *The Popcorn Report*) its mission would be to respond to the expressed needs of local levels of volunteer community service to further the cause of volunteerism, and it would continually find creative ways to take the pulse of those local levels to insure that its' responsiveness was "on the money". Its action plans would be written in pencil in the anticipation of changing needs and it's flexibility to respond with quality efforts would be its greatest strength.

I believe that such a group will begin with only a limited number of programs although they will offer more as time goes on and will include training efforts to equip local leaders with practical tools for activism; a standards and ethics division which would offer certification based on competency as measured by established criteria, and ethics guidelines & audits for program management; think-tanks to challenge people to devise better and better ways to accomplish agreed-on goals; and an advocacy "response team" to keep tabs on legislative and corporate issues which require the perspective of the voluntary sector.

In 1991, the Points of Light Foundation (POLF), which the year before had merged with VOLUNTEER: The National Center (and which has as part of its family the National Council on Corporate Volunteerism and Council of Volunteer Centers), initiated a project titled "The Changing Paradigm".

This project sought to find ways to increase the impact of community service, both on the organizations served and on the volunteers themselves. Specifically POLF wished to learn more about what are perceived to be "barriers" to the most effective involvement of volunteers.

In the first year, the initial research phase was implemented to learn about factors that either facilitated or inhibited the effectiveness of volunteering in nonprofit and public sector "human service organizations", a definition which included schools, educational programs, hospitals and health care organizations, social service groups and grass-roots, community-based organizations.

Over 400 people in twenty such organizations in various communities were interviewed. Both paid staff and volunteers were asked specific questions about effectiveness of volunteer involvement, and as the research began to pile up, it became quite clear that some of the organizations were doing a better job involving volunteers than others.

In these outstanding organizations, it was noted that the work of their volunteers was more directly contributing to the mission and priorities of the organization; there were fewer tensions between paid staff and volunteers; there was a greater breadth and depth to their involvement; and there was less resistance to change and innovation in the roles played by volunteers.

The analysis of the interviews identified eleven "characteristics of high effectiveness" that differentiated these organizations from the others examined. These characteristics were:

1. *The mission and priorities of the organization are framed in terms of the problem or issue the organization is addressing, not its short-range institutional concerns.*

2. *There is a positive vision-clearly articulated, widely-shared and openly discussed throughout the organization-of the role of volunteers.*

3. *Volunteers are seen as valuable human resources that can directly contribute to achievement of the organizations' mission, not primarily as a means to obtaining financial or other material resources.*

4. *Leaders at all levels, policy-making, executive and middle-management, work in concert to encourage and facilitate high impact volunteer involvement.*

5. *There is a clear focal point of leadership for volunteering but the volunteer management function is well-integrated at all levels and in all parts of the organization.*

6. *Paid staff are respected and are empowered to fully participate in planning, decision-making and management related to volunteer involvement.*

7. *There is a conscious, active effort to reduce the boundaries and increase the teamwork between paid and volunteer staff.*

8. *Potential barriers to volunteer involvement-liability, confidentiality, location of the organization, hours of operation, etc.-are identified and are dealt with forthrightly.*

9. *Success breeds success as stories of the contributions of volunteers-both historically and currently-are shared among both paid and volunteer staff.*

10. *There is an openness to the possibility for change, an eagerness to improve performance and conscious, organized efforts to learn from and about volunteers' experiences in the organization.*

11. *There is a recognition of the value of involving, as volunteers, people from all segments of the community, including those the organization seeks to serve.*

In the second year, the project was expanded to acquire feedback on the report and to gather comments and suggestions for next steps. Those steps include the development and field-testing of tools and training programs to put the research into practical use, so that agencies can learn from the characteristics of successful organizations and can replicate that success in their own.

Specific Volunteer Centers around the country will act as test locations for training programs to help agencies affiliated with them benefit from the research and to find the tools to help groups attain maximum effectiveness.

The second year also helped gather responses to the eleven characteristics, to flesh out greater detail for each, and categorize them into four "action principles". This clustering will help groups hone in on over-riding principles which must be present for the most effective involvement of volunteers in organizations.

The four principles are:
1. Lay the foundation through mission and vision.
2. Combine inspiring leadership with effective management.
3. Build understanding and collaboration.
4. Learn, grow and change.

As you read through this book and note trends shaping our world, you will be struck by how "on target" these four principles

---

are in relationship to what Americans are saying they want and need.

The Changing the Paradigm project is simply one excellent example of what a national organization can do to provide direct service to local communities as they go about the business of serving their local needs. The process by which this project was implemented is a good example of 'partnering' with grassroots groups, i.e.: Volunteer Centers, to insure direct responsiveness to local perspectives and needs.

FUNDING

The major clan-gatherer group's funding would come from members, supporters, foundations, governments and product sales and services (program evaluations, development, training, conferences, etc.). It would not, however, be beholden to any special interest groups or individuals or be associated with only one political party.

Such a group may sound a bit far-fetched in early 1990's, but beneath all this author's white hair lurks a true optimist and enough of a left-brain to believe that the need for such a visionary organization and clan-gatherer is so clear as to inspire one of the current groups to re-mold themselves to respond to our needs.

MISSION DRIVEN

This group will be driven by their mission, and articulate it internally, measuring everything against it for compatibility. Every action, effort and communication will be an embodiment of the mission and new people who come to work within its fold will be required to fully understand what the group is all about.

In addition to keeping the organization honest, the practice of measuring everything against its stated mission will serve as a model to other groups and help them replicate this "mission-driven" philosophy. Internally, the focus on where the group hopes to go will assist them in long range planning, and once again, serve as a model for other groups planning for the future.

"LEADERSHIFT" AND "RELATIONAL MANAGEMENT"

In Chapter 10 of this book, I have explained in detail the principles of what I have dubbed "Leadershift" and "Relational Management". To offer you a quick glimpse of what I mean by those phrases, let me give you rather simple definitions:

"Leadership": _The ability to move people in and out of process circles as projects demand._

"Relational Management": _The working relationship between people and the process, work, mission and others._

Our primary group or clan-gatherer will embody both of these philosophies, using them to effectively operate internally, and again, to serve as a model for groups with which they interact.

Using Leadershift, the group will assess the goal of various work assignments to determine what is needed to achieve that goal. Then they will decide who logically might bring to the work circle the expertise, experience or perspective needed to accomplish the stated goal.

Next it will identify and assemble the people thought to be needed, sharing the vision of the work project and asking for what these people feel could be their role in such a project. Leadershift understands that it is not enough that an organization's leaders see a role for a particular individual; that individual must _also_ see their role in the effort and "buy into" it.

When agreement has been reached between all parties to be involved, Leadershift swings into high gear as each group member articulates their vision of the goal, their role in the effort and determines how all the perspectives fit together. Again and again, during these first discussions, work is measured against the mission of the organization and the goal of the project.

72

The Emergence of a National Leadership Group

As the work begins, each member of the group has a turn when their expertise, experience or perspective is critical. At that point, they do indeed become the "leader" of the group and all the other people stand ready to allow the leadership role to **shift** to them, respecting them for their contribution and knowledge.

The work itself is carried out through Relational Management, whereby the person ultimately responsible for the project focuses on systems that empower workers for productive relationships between people, work, others, self and the mission of the organization. Going much deeper than simply the "climate" of the organization, Relational Management is sensitive to how things are meshing, how well systems are furthering the work and insuring that nothing is blocking the process.

Like an artist carefully watching the overall design of a painting or the orchestra leader focused on the total sound of the combined instruments, those who utilize Relational Management will pay close attention to the synthesization and relationships among all the various parts of the effort. Groups and individuals who adopt this management philosophy will use flexibility, adaptability and TRUST as their foundations for interaction, drawing together communities within a community to achieve stated and specific goals that further the general mission.

Leadershift will guide overall organizational efforts, with group participants moving on to new assignments, created again by the logical gathering of those who can contribute to a new work goal. It may be that the configuration of people gathered together to lead any one particular effort may not be together again for a long time.........common sense and logic sets the stage for work teams rather than little boxes on a management chart. They also determine timings for interaction......it is not necessary for a person to sit in on every meeting when what they have to contribute is not effected by or interactive with what is being discussed at that time....simple minutes of such meetings will suffice.

The national group which will lead our field into the next century will adopt such a philosophy, leading its own staff and gathering together other groups in a community-building cooperative to achieve wider goals for the good of the citizenry served by such coordinated and empowering efforts.

TREND-TRACKER

Such a national clan gatherer will continually have its antenna up for new trends in the field of volunteer community service and external trends that will impact how work will be done and funds raised for our field. Volunteerism and philanthropy will be tied even closer as the decade folds itself into the new century.

The group will need to find ways to measure all layers of our sector, which by its very nature, is multi-faced. (Peter Drucker who first referred to our unique segment of America as the "Independent Sector" now seems to be calling it the "Service Sector". Choose what you wish to title who we all are, remembering that we are incredibly varied and diverse.)

Some of the trends which should impact what this group does in allocations of time, energy and resources include:

1. ***A growing population of retired people and seniors*** (not all retired folks will be seniors...more and more people are finding ways to retire at an earlier age) will become a deepening resource for volunteer community service. How to best tap this resource and connect into its ranks will be a major challenge. Our clan-gatherer would encourage groups to prepare pre-retirement programs to try to lock in commitments prior to the point at which workers will have more disposable time to offer as well as financial resources such as gifts and bequeaths.

2. ***International changes*** in governments, alliances, economic coalitions etc. will open doors of opportunity for groups to expand their impact around the globe. Our major clan-gatherer will recognize this trend and be a major factor in spreading the gospel of voluntarism around the world. It will personally have several international programs, and work closely with groups who have like agenda.

3. ***Worker satisfaction*** for both paid and volunteer workers will become a dominant factor in the next few decades, and our leader group will help others understand this and build healthy climates and support for workers. They will lead the efforts to measure such satisfaction and even create tools to help groups assess how workers are feeling about their efforts. Assessments,

audits and evaluations will become a major effort into the 21st century, as people demand ways to measure effectiveness of groups and volunteers, and then decide whether or not to become involved with specific organizations.   People want their energies to be spent wisely and will avoid those groups which do not return appropriate value for their investment!

4. **Time** will continue to dominate decisions people make on how to spend this most valuable asset. A recent study by the Hilton Hotel chain on time allocation revealed that workers would be willing to give up a day's pay to have more time to spend with family or by themselves. Our national group will help others focus on time-efficiency.

5. In part because of this value of time, **flexible work options** will be supported by our group and again, modeled to other organizations. Volunteers and paid staff will do work from home linked by computer, FAX, modem and other technological advances that allow assignments to be accomplished creatively and non-traditionally.

6. As **self-help groups proliferate,** ways will be found to embrace them in the fold of the national community service circle. Because their role in our society is unique to very specific missions, and because their focus is rarely on organizational development, our creative clan-gatherer will have to explore new ways to interact with them to provide information they might need to operate their own, independent efforts most effectively.

Our national group will see strong growth in numbers of associates when a continual, open and flexible method is found to embrace such self-help and other entrepreneurial groups into its fold.   When this occurs, mutual respect will replace any previous lack of appreciation of each other and bridge the false premise exhibited for many years that there is nothing organized groups can learn from "spontaneous, grassroots" entities.

When the relationship is established, everyone will benefit as large and sophisticated national and international organizations interact with the most loosely organized efforts working to impact a singular issue of our society. The small groups can absorb tools, learnings and assistance from the larger groups, while those same large organizations can benefit from being reminded of how much passionate commitment can help people accomplish incredible things through direct, creative solutions to problems!

7. **Religion is changing** in the American society, with so-called Baby Boomers returning to centers of faith in record numbers or creating their own spiritual communities that reflect their values and beliefs. The wise clan-gatherer will see this vast untapped potential as part of the total picture of volunteer community service, EVEN IF THE RELIGIOUS COMMUNITY DOES NOT RECOGNIZE THEIR CONNECTION at first!

Our super-group will find ways to communicate our similarities, focusing on ways that partnerships would be mutually beneficial. I would expect that at first, only those groups would become connected which have the capacity to focus on commonalties and ignore differences. Groups that insist everyone involved with them must embrace their specific doctrine will probably not become part of the larger community brought together by this clan-gatherer. Those that do not have such a demand will find ways to interact and benefit from new collaborative relationships, finding new avenues of service and a new platform for their voice. Once again, we would all benefit from their inclusion and partnering.

Churches put nearly half of the money they receive into charitable use and nine out of ten of the nation's congregations have one or more programs in human service and welfare according to a survey from Independent Sector, thus pointing to a logical inclusion of churches to our "field". Churches also represent the larger trend toward the melding of volunteerism and philanthropy and thus serve as a model for how the two can best work together in service.

8. According to Peter Francese, founder of American Demographics magazine, the **three key themes of the 1990s** that will impact nonprofits most dramatically include a focus of concern for community & family with special attention to solving local problems; the demand by the public in general and Baby Boomers in particular for solid information about who the organization is, what unique service they provide and how they

are using contributor's money to do good, and the move toward being information-based in the management of their operations (the assessment demand mentioned previously).

Based on these three trends, all major groups of American volunteerism and philanthropy will need to correlate their choices of programs and efforts to respond to these issues. Without this correlation, some good projects may fail because they are not perceived as either needed, responsive or open about their way of doing business.

9. **An *infusion of volunteers from the workplace*** will bring about different expectations for logistical support as they go about their work. Being used to such support in their paid work settings, they will expect the same in their voluntary surroundings also. Groups, led by our clan-gatherer, will have to produce solid materials, kits and workbooks for their non-paid staff to use as they go about their work.

   This expectation will become a real need of workers and cause our nationally-effective group to become even more in tune with what is needed "in the trenches" at the same time that they are reaching out to the highest levels of organizations......a stretch in two directions that will be difficult in the process, but richly rewarding in its accomplishment. This stretch will create a natural internal diversity that will actually strengthen the super-group's voice, clout, understanding and viability with all segments of our society......sort of the "Paul Bunyan/Ninja Turtle" profile!

10. There will be an **increased *competition for volunteers*** by any name, and the national groups which win the greatest followings will be those that help organizations stretch their volunteer resources further or encourage new pockets of potential volunteers to be uncovered and tapped. The major national group will understand that this is not simply a numbers game.... "just tell us how to recruit MORE volunteers".....but rather, one of helping groups use the resources they have available more wisely and effectively, especially through the development of cooperatives, coalition, information sharing and creative partnering arrangements.

Megatrends & Volunteerism

This book is dedicated to looking at trends and saying "so what?" to voluntary community service. The ten trends mentioned here are simply those most appropriately focused on in this section as we talk about an emerging national leader group. As you read trends in other sections, ask yourself how they might apply to your own organization and how they might influence our super-group and clan-gatherer through the years.

THE CRIES FROM THE TRENCHES

There is an increasing list of concerns from people at the grassroots, get-it-done, we-need-it-now trenches, to which any national group must be responsive.

As I interact with agency CEOs, program directors, consultants and leaders of voluntary community service initiatives, I am hearing complaints and frustrations. They include:

"The national level of my organization doesn't seem to understand the real issues we deal with in volunteerism and community service."

"The headquarters of my organization seems to believe that our purpose is to support their office rather than to serve the clients. Sometimes I feel as if they think the survival of their building, meetings, staff and materials is what we are all about rather than the survival of the people afflicted with (disease)."

"Our leadership talks about collaborative efforts, then makes decisions that effect us without telling us or letting us have input into to their conclusions."

"No one at the national level seems to understand that simply recruiting MORE volunteers is not the answer."

"People give answers that are too simplistic to truly address our complex issues."

"Why doesn't the national leadership understand that when they heap yet another project or demand on our already overloaded schedules, we can't drop everything to get it done. Their time frames are unrealistic."

The Emergence of a National Leadership Group

"Our larger agency seems to be intent on letting our volunteer department die of benign neglect."

"The national group I belong to is so territorial they spend most of their time guarding their turf and little time helping us do a better job."

"Where do I turn for help? They're so busy starting pilot programs and getting grants that they don't develop practical tools for me to use in my daily job."

"Why doesn't the leadership understand that we all have something to contribute...they only talk to a few of the field leaders and forget the rest of us. Talking to the same people over and over again only offers selected perspectives. There is more to the challenges we face than what someone from New York city or Los Angeles can understand."

The challenge for a truly responsive and credible leader group will be to find ways to hear the concerns from the trenches, be they in Manhattan or Menomenee Falls, Peoria or Pine Bluff.

Such a group will need to address those which are real and possible to impact, and interact with leaders who can offer honest perspectives to help them devise appropriate responses. I would suggest that one way to do this would be to involve those people most credible to those trenches, their own niche leaders or authenticators, who can help bridge any gaps between the national landscape and that of the grassroots levels.

A leader group must emerge that can gather together all the facets of volunteerism into a safe, ethical and empowering community which seeks to shape the American agenda of the future.

Chapter 5

INTERNATIONAL EXPANSION & INCLUSION

"At the core... is a belief that free and effective societies exist in direct proportion to their degree of citizen participation and influence."
.......Brian O'Connell, James Joseph. CIVICUS Fact Sheet.

"Our task...is to find the few principles that will calm the infinite anguish of free souls. We must mend what has been torn apart, make justice imaginable again in a world so obviously unjust, give happiness a meaning once more... It is a superhuman task. But superhuman is the term for tasks (that) take a long time to accomplish, that's all."
......Albert Camus

This particular chapter will probably be the shortest in this book, yet have the longest effect in the field of volunteerism.

New horizons have opened up with the collapse of the Berlin wall, USSR and communism in so many eastern European countries, plus the growth of the European common market, nationalism and increased demands for democratic governance world-wide, that a whole new world surrounds us.

In 1989, Senator David Pryor of Arkansas was involved in discussions regarding actions America might take to help emerging nations seeking democracy, and suggested that what we most needed to export was our volunteerism know-how.

How right he was.

We are now in a time when nations at all stages of development recognize their need to introduce voluntary actions and citizen participation into their country's changing dynamics. To this end, a new international alliance has been formed to provide a structure where those working in nonprofit, non governmental, and philanthropic activities from many countries can communicate and learn from each other.

These first actions, in addition to those of volunteer program managers united through the International Association for Volunteer Efforts (IAVE) and interested parties who attend the Association for Volunteer Administration's annual International Conference on Volunteerism, point to a megatrend mentioned by every major trend-watcher: **a new, global perspective.**

This perspective is advanced through another trend that has become apparent:

Volunteerism through citizen involvement has been identified as a motivating and defining force behind the successful integration of democracy, and is therefore of heightened interest as our globe redefines itself.

The combination of these two paradigm shifts in thinking, create a foundation for the expansion of volunteerism internationally and the inclusion of leaders from the global community as we map the future of our field.

America is known around the world as a country founded on volunteerism, and its basic tenants are so ingrained in all we do, we are naturally being turned to as resources to bring our spirit of citizen involvement to the rest of the world.

CIVICUS

Brian O'Connell, President of Independent Sector, along with James A. Joseph, President of the Council on Foundations, led an effort in the first part of the 1990s to form an international alliance to promote active citizenship, pluralism, voluntary action and private philanthropy.

The effort, which culminated in **CIVICUS: World Alliance for Citizen Participation**, held its first meeting in May of 1993 in Spain and called for its first World Assembly in December of 1994. Nineteen countries were represented during the first two years of fact finding and deliberation. Their mission was to discover how best to provide a meeting ground for voluntary organizations, funding groups and others throughout the world who want to find ways to develop greater citizen involvement around the globe.

CIVICUS has set lofty goals of influencing the world order by helping countries and leaders truly understand the impact and positive power of volunteerism in all facets of development and growth. Participants include regional, national and international organizations devoted to strengthening voluntary initiatives; private funding organizations interested in helping build voluntary and philanthropic activity; plus international, regional and national associations whose primary interest may be program-specific, but who understand the need to help build a climate for greater voluntarism and philanthropy throughout their nation.

I share all this with you simply because it is a classic and wonderful example of response to a megatrend that already has us in its grip. The global perspective will influence everything we do as a field, from several different perspectives.

TRANSFERRING OUR NORTH AMERICAN EXPERTISE

Because America, and all of North America through our Canadian colleagues, has developed volunteerism, volunteer administration and program leadership to such a fine art, it is natural for the rest of the world to look to us for help as they expand existing efforts or seek to take the first, tentative steps toward introducing citizen participation to their homeland.

In a recent visit to Russia, a colleague and dear friend, Elaine Yarbrough, Ph.D., worked with factory managers who sought skills of worker-negotiation. She was startled to realize that before there could be any discussion of negotiating skills, she had to step back to simply explain the **concept** of communicating needs and the exchange of value for value.

Those who have ventured into countries where volunteerism has never reached beyond the most grass-roots forms of helping a relative plow a field, find that the **concept** of citizen participation is so foreign as to be beyond comprehension!

Our task, therefore, in helping to bring volunteerism to others globally, will not simply be one of teaching volunteer management principles. Instead we will need to begin with an explanation of what volunteering is on a citizen-organized, rather than personal and spontaneous, level. Until we can help others catch sight of the vision of what citizen participation can be, we cannot go beyond to the intricacies of program development, management, marketing, or leadership.

Simply translating our existing body of knowledge into various languages just won't cut it! Nor will the opening of our American training conferences to international visitors be a quick answer to their needs. What we offer will have to go much deeper, beginning with a conceptual understanding of what we are all about.

I can recall that when I was with Project Concern and visiting one of our most rural programs providing medical and dental health services in Appalachia, I was struck by a story of a young patient, who needed extensive dental care. Before she was willing to consent to having a dentist examine her, however, she had to be **introduced to the fact that there was a doctor who worked just on teeth.** Until she was convinced that such an unheard of concept was true, she would have no part of anyone looking inside her mouth!

To share an even greater insight as to how foreign the whole concept of dental hygiene was to her, let me also tell you that after several months of treatment, her mother rushed this girl, who was hysterical, to the dental clinic van one morning. Why the hysteria?....because she had awakened to experience NO pain in her teeth or gums, and she was sure something was wrong!

"But I always thought teeth was supposed to hurt," she told our dental hygienist in disbelief.

International Expansion & Inclusion

A classic example of the most basic conceptual foundations needed for understanding.

It also illustrates the basic levels to which we, who are so accustomed to volunteerism, may have to go to help global colleagues still struggling with the UN-experienced concept of people voluntarily working for the betterment of the wider community. How ironic, that those raised under the banner of "communism" will find it most foreign.

I would expect that over the next decade and well into the first half of the 21st century, volunteer program executives will receive calls and requests from all over the world for shared expertise and basic "how to" information in every variety of program.

Where before you may have had inquiries from colleagues working in similar efforts in neighboring cities or states, you will now get calls from far away countries; where now you mingle at international conferences with like-missioned leaders from Maine and Mississippi, you will now cluster with additional folks from Moscow and Madrid.

As this happens, we in American and Canadian programs, will play the role of expert, sharing resources, information and tips to help our global colleagues as they set up their own programs. At the same time, I am hopeful that we will not miss the opportunity to learn from these newcomers, as they ask their questions, pose their own solutions and explain the different nuances they must deal with in establishing efforts.

Like the inexperienced child who is uninhibited by prejudice and unaware of "impossibilities", they may often provide new perspectives and insights to long-standing challenges with which we have struggled. Many times, wisdom and common-sense answers come from those unencumbered with "expertise", such as the young soldier after the 1992 gulf war, who happened to be around as experts in oil rig fires discussed the weeks of frustration they had experienced in attempting to shut down one particularly stubborn well.

"Why not just shut the valve off?" he suggested.

Stunned with the simplicity of this solution, they tried it and you guessed it, it worked!

In our desire to be helpful experts, we might find a wealth of great wisdom as we listen to newcomers in our field suggesting common-sense ways to accomplish their dreams!

"HAVE FLIP-CHART; WILL TRAVEL"

Another facet of volunteerism that will be effected, is that peculiar group of people known as national trainers and consultants. This merry band, geared to one-day appearances at training seminars, and far too familiar with Holiday Inns, airports with hot dogs rolling around on warmer grills and grabbed between flights, will probably need an international OAG (Official Airline Guide).

Instead of trying to figure out how to get from Peoria to Portland on a Tuesday evening, they will have to plan for a little more leeway (and jet lag) as they hop from Peoria to Prague or Chicago to Cairo.

A whole new cluster of trainers and consultants will emerge, who are willing to take on the challenge of international travel and all the work it will take to gather background information on the country and its people's customs before tackling the translations needed to bring volunteerism and management to those who so desperately need it.

Flexibility will be a necessary trait of anyone attempting to take on such contracts, as they work to retro-fit information that worked in Boston for the needs of those in Bonn.

INTERNATIONAL INCLUSION IN VOLUNTEER CONFERENCES

Both the Points of Light Foundation (formerly VOLUNTEER) and the Association for Volunteer Administration, have made a concerted efforts in the past decade to include international participants in their annual conferences. This trend will grow, and I would predict that by the year 2000, almost every group holding an annual conference, be they an association, charity, university or philanthropic entity, will provide opportunities for inclusion of global colleagues.

86

International Expansion & Inclusion

More than offering tokenism, workshops and plenaries will offer solid learning, sharing and information for international participants. Those of us from America and Canada will also find opportunities to learn from these same global community leaders as they address issues in their homeland.

As the international expansion of volunteerism circles the earth, and as we include global partners in our community of citizen participation in areas as diverse as arts and zoos, health and the environment, we will all benefit from new levels of sharing and communication.

By putting our heads together, we will discover the commonalties of concern and identify global issues that effect us all, whether we live in America or Russia or South Africa or Newfoundland, and then build communities of action around those issues to make the earth a healthier, safer and more hospitable place in which to live.

Although this is the shortest chapter of this work, it casts the furthest reaching, most profound and long-lasting shadow of effect on our future. International expansion and inclusion of volunteerism and volunteer administration, will redefine how we work, think, act and react to the challenges before us.

By sharing what we know to this point, and being willing to listen to the new enthusiasm and determination of yet-unmet colleagues from far and away, we will grow and expand our horizons in unheard of ways that will benefit us all.

In the wonderful little book, "Jonathan Livingston Seagull", author Richard Bach tells us that:

"The gull sees furthest who flies highest".

Those in our field who reach for the horizon of international understanding and expansion will indeed fly highest and see furthest, to a world made better through the care of those embracing the voluntary spirit and putting that spirit into action.

**We're broadening our horizons, and
becoming the richer because of it.**

Megatrends & Volunteerism

Chapter 6

ETHICS AND
PUBLIC PERCEPTION

"The important thing to remember (is) you've got to be accountable to the people. The issue is your knowledge that you tried to do the right thing.".
...Attorney General Janet Reno

"In this day and age, voluntary organizations have to practice a wide degree of openness and full disclosure so that there is no suspicion or doubt about the way the organization is functioning and no lack of access to information by which people can make fair judgments....the public expects the highest values and ethics to be practiced habitually in nonprofit organizations."
...Brian O'Connell,
"For Voluntary Organizations In Trouble Or Don't Want To Be"

In 1992 and 1993, at exactly the same time that Faith Popcorn in her *Popcorn Report* was speaking at length about the trend toward ethical behavior and responsibility, the results of an investigation into the financial affairs of the CEO of United Way of America revealed some questionable expenditures.

The timing could not have been worse.....or more symbolic!

As cries of "foul" echoed from the public and local United Ways which belonged to UWA (not all do), the CEO left under pressure.

What followed was a wave of high scrutiny of salaries and benefits for executives of nonprofits that still rages today and has put a laser beam of light on details of how public service agencies are perceived to spend their dollars and energies.

The United Way story remained in the headlines for so long that its effect was felt by all manner of groups. New phrases such as 'ethics audit'" began to creep into our vocabulary and a few less-than-reputable executives took early retirements or became consultants in order to escape investigation.

Sadly, the negative effect of the United Way of America story resulted in a fallout that took few prisoners, especially local United Ways which are independent from UWA (it is essentially a trade organization) and extremely judicious in their spending activities.

Other groups, equally innocent of any wrong-doing, found major funders withdrawing pledges and resources. To compound the problem, individual donors followed suit and moneys from them dropped dramatically.

All of this is simply symbolic of a growing demand from the public for ethical behavior from those who run institutions, businesses and other public trust organizations. Cynicism in America is at an all-time high, and poll after poll reveals a basic distrust of bureaucracies, organizations and institutions. The public perception is not overwhelmed with good feelings toward many groups!

This in turn plays itself out by people looking for ways to check on ethics and values in groups before they make any contributions of time, money or energy.

The megatrend focusing on ethics and public perception is one of three issues which many writers believe will shape the last decade of the 20th century and carry over into the 21st:

Ethics   Ecology   Education

Even though writers such as John Naisbitt, Tom Peters, Peter Drucker, Faith Popcorn and a dozen others may have used different terms for this age of accountability, all referred to it as a major, underlying trend.

The executives in charge of volunteer programs will be called on by regulatory agencies, the public, media, administration, funders and other interested parties to offer proof of ethical behavior and use of resources.

As I've said many times before: **Accountability is IN, and Arrogance is OUT!**

Arrogant tyrants have fallen like dead ducks in the last decade of the 20th century and found themselves jailed, disgraced, fined and fired in varying degrees. I find it interesting to note that none of them view what they did as wrong and often are stunned that they are being held accountable for their actions. Whether from the arena of evangelism, government, savings and loans, the hotel industry, sports, religion, education or business, they seem dumbfounded that they are being forced to adhere to the same standards as "the little people".

But that's exactly what's happening; the public is demanding that the same rules of ethical behavior and accountability be applied to every citizen....whether they drive the bus or own the company, have a net worth of $100 or $100 million, were elected to the PTA or national office.

In the area of compensation of nonprofit or public executives, many misconceptions exist which in the long run can hinder the volunteer component of the agency, thus affecting you as the volunteer program executive.

More directly, you may want to help your administration sort through the ethical factors which must go into compensation decisions for nonprofit executives and professionals and the public perceptions of same. The best source I know of to help you with this is a booklet by Brian O'Connell and E.B. Knauft, the President and former Executive VP of Independent Sector, titled *Financial Compensation in Nonprofit Organizations.*

I'll let you read the 26 page offering on your own but will give you a glimpse of the four factors Brian addresses in his opening chapter:

"Compensation in the nonprofit sector represents four very different problems:

☞ *First, some salaries and other compensation arrangements are egregiously high.*

☞ *"Second, some compensation arrangements appear to be high because too little effort has been made to interpret what it takes to attract and hold people who can lead large and complex voluntary institutions.*

☞ *"Third, there is an incorrect but pervasive interpretation that salaries are overhead.*

☞ *"Fourth, and most severe, most salaries and benefits in nonprofit organizations are so low as to threaten development and maintenance of essential activities.*

All four problems require urgent attention."

The best way to characterize the attention to ethical behavior is to view it as someone looking over our shoulders every day in every area. For those who have always been ethical and above-board, the scrutiny will hopefully bring praise and honor. For those who bend rules, shave the truth, rearrange numbers or act in any other, even subtle, unethical ways, the scrutiny will bring retribution and punishment of varying degrees.

I have found that the vast majority of volunteer program executives are more than ethical, tending to put their own money in the till rather than a hand taking it out! Do not, however, think that the ethics issue is only a monetary one. Far beyond that, the demand for ethics covers how we treat people, especially volunteers, when interacting with them; how we use or abuse time and energy offered by workers; how closely we stick to the mission of the organization; how we treat colleagues and co-workers; how we interact with the earth around us, being careful not to abuse its bounty, etc. etc.

The megatrend surrounding the issue of ethics is much wider and deeper than most people believe. Being 'good' most of the time won't cut it anymore. Excuses won't be tolerated or allowances made for any category....not clergy, not children, not bosses, not celebrities or anyone else, no matter what their status. If their actions are unethical, they will answer for their choices of action and pay for the consequences.

As our Pastor told each of our son's confirmation classes when discussing life's choices:

> *"You are free to choose. You are NOT free to choose the consequences."*
>
> ....Pastor Hollis Bishop

AUDITS

No, not the kind done by a CPA with a green eye-shade and squinty eyes, but an audit to insure that the organization is continually moving toward its mission and that the human, financial and energy resources available are working toward that same mission.

This 'audit' will become a common occurrence by the turn of the century as people hold corporations, agencies and individuals accountable for all that they do......especially when it involves public or private money and the use of volunteers!

Sloppy utilization of the volunteer resources of energy, time, creativity, gifts and skills will no more be tolerated than sloppy bookkeeping. Exorbitant CEO salaries will not be acceptable nor will mis-use of volunteers. The days of 'recruitment by slight-of-hand' and 'retention-by-guilt' are over, and any group that attempts to continue such suicidal methods will probably find itself shuttering its offices.

Organizations must audit themselves and programs must do the same to be able to offer the public, including donors and volunteers, solid information to show that they are indeed being true to their mission. Audits must be done honestly and with no prejudice so that a true assessment is made.

To become more effective, this audit needs to be done from the natural, varied perspectives of different entities touched by it: administrators, policy makers, workers, paid and volunteer staff, suppliers, clients, the general public, managers. Examination must also be made of projects, departments and specific efforts to "audit" their effectiveness and directions.

In response to the growing demands for accountability, criteria must be agreed on at the start of any assessment so a basis for measurement can be used fairly. This may be harder than one might think as the age-old dilemma arises of whether to measure a human service by the number of clients served or the quality of the service seen in long-term results.

If you had always thought of audits as something only the accounting department had to worry about, take another look. Every trend book in America today points to the issue of accountability and a growing cry for solid data on which to make decisions of support and involvement.......translation: "prove you will use my energy or dollars wisely!".

CHANGE

After an honest audit, organizations will need to take the following, sometimes difficult steps:

1. Abandon things that do not work, the things that have never worked; the things that have outlived their usefulness and their capacity to contribute.

2. Concentrate on the things that do work; the things that produce results; the things that improve the organization's ability to perform.

3. Analyze half-successes and half-failures. Shelve or drop those that cannot be salvaged or be made successful enough to matter.

Again, **MEASURE ALL OF THIS INFORMATION AGAINST THE MISSION!**

94

For organizations to survive and thrive into the 21st century, strong measures will need to be taken to assess and then remedy problems while building on strengths. Though many might categorize this type of re-alignment to the mission under the heading of Organizational Dynamics, it really is seen by the public as an ethical issue of being true to what you have said your mission is.

THE SUBTLE ISSUES OF ETHICAL BEHAVIOR

When speaking about ethics, it is easy to focus attention on grossly unethical behavior such as: stealing, immoral conduct, dis-information, lying, favoritism, nepotism, illegal acts, sexual harassment, misuse of property or assets, etc.

Obviously, these must be addressed, but there are other, far more subtle forms of unethical behavior that I believe can creep into our organizations and be 'over-looked' too frequently. It is this category that I believe does the most damage to groups because it erodes trust and sends a whispering campaign out to potential volunteers and donors that the group should be avoided. I also believe these subtle killers do much to add to burnout of paid staff and volunteers as they have to divert energies to deal with them.

All have to do with personal integrity. It is not enough, for example, that a person refrains from stealing large sums from the treasury, he or she must also refrain from fudging on expense accounts or stealing ideas from others.

The ethical person does not ever:

Bad-mouth colleagues, even casually, in conversations with others. The higher a person's position the more carefully they must measure their words. Besides realizing that such personal smears put them in line for slander suits, they recognize that such actions are highly unethical. Who would be part of an organization led by such people?

Withhold information needed by others for success. Good decisions are based on the most extensive information possible

95

and for anyone to intentionally keep such data from those who need it, is, I believe, a deeply repugnant and unethical action.

Take credit for another's action. I was recently told about a hospital volunteer coordinator who had a great fundraising idea. She shared it with the Auxiliary President who in turn presented it to the Director of Development. This person promptly discounted it as impractical.

Imagine the surprise of both the DVS and President when, several months later, the Director of Development unveiled "his" new fund raising idea and they recognized it as the DVS's!

The idea was successful, the DD got applause and a raise, the Director of Volunteer Services is talking about early retirement and the Auxiliary President has left to work with the Historical Society!

Give 'dis-information'. **Mis**information is information shared that is thought to be correct. **DIS**information is information shared that is known to be false. It is frequently given to undermine or do harm to another individual or effort. Having once been the target of such disinformation, I can tell you personally how disheartening and energy-draining fighting it can be. Unethical? Yes, and frustrating too.

Saying "yes", meaning "no". Ethical leaders do not promise to do one thing and then do another, or say they will take action when they really have no such intention.

I once worked for a CEO who assured me he would take care of a personnel problem of which he said he had been unaware. He never did and I later found out many people had alerted him to the same problem, elicited a promise to take action immediately, but they, along with me, never saw action on it. He promised what he had no intention of doing.

Kill creative thinking. In another section of this book, I speak to the 'Founder Syndrome", in which someone who has founded an organization or devised a program is violently opposed to any change in what they have created. It is not unusual for some of these founders to kill any creative suggestions that might alter "their" effort. Sadly they often react this way because they have their own significance confused with their effort.

I was called in once by a manager of a symphony orchestra, who was dumbfounded by the resistance she constantly met from one specific board member whenever any suggestions came up about changes in the symphony's annual Christmas program.

The manager had been with the group only 18 months, so I asked her to research when the first Christmas program had been held and who was in charge. She called me after a week, and already had the answer to her question on resistance. Sure enough, the board member who fought every effort to alter the program was indeed the founding chair of the event, and had to fight long and hard for her all-baroque evening.

For several years the board member had chaired the event (before a paid manager was part of the organization), and had received recognition and even celebrity status in her community for her efforts. The manager and I talked about what happens when someone sees a program they began as their major significance, and begins to confuse their worth with their work.

This was obviously the case with the symphony board member, and she was determined to shoot down any suggestions that might alter what she considered to be her personal triumph, the Christmas program. We then discussed ways to help this founder retain her significance while still being able to update the event.

In close consultation with the Board Chair, the manager chose to suggest naming the christmas event for the founding board member as a permanent tribute to her contribution to the community. It was a sincere thank you, and pleased the founder, who then allowed changes to be introduced to the program a year later.

Blocking creative thinking for personal reasons is not only unethical, it is very dangerous to an organization or cause. Creative people will leave settings where they are punished for original thinking, and organizations without fresh approaches and creative thinking will eventually die on the vine.

Work for peace at any price. (also known as the "Nice Lady Syndrome") Though many might argue that any effort to promote peace could not be unethical, I'd argue back that some varieties can be most hazardous to the health of any effort or relationship and **highly** unethical.

Those who seek to keep peace by refusing to confront or even admit to the existence of conflicts, are being unethical in the sense that they are not being honest. Pretending all is well when it really isn't, is really no different than closing one's eyes as others steal from the cash register!

Healthy organizations see problems as challenges and opportunities to learn. They spend their energies seeking solutions rather than denying problems. Being ethical means being honest... even when problems arise.

Work to blame. Ethical people spend time analyzing problems and finding solutions. They do not waste time looking for and crucifying scapegoats. Personal attacks rank high on the list of unethical behaviors.

Set others up for failure. Unfortunately, there are lots of ways to do this. Some time ago I worked with a conference chair who wanted me to train for her in the Chicago area, where I live.

When I accepted, she seemed almost disappointed. This reaction made me keep my antenna up for other strange responses from her, and I was not surprised when they came time and time again:

☞ She kept delaying a decision on the meeting space, until it was too late to a get suitable site.

☞ She "forgot" to mail requests for program suggestions to the program committee.

☞ Job assignments were so complex and over-lapping as to insure failure.

☞ When the copy for the registration brochure was finished it was delayed dramatically for 'proofing', and she demanded inconsequential changes, holding it up it even more.

The conference did happen, but in the most confused, anger-filled atmosphere possible, with far less attendees than anticipated, in a setting inappropriate for the training topic (wellness) and inconvenient for everyone involved.

A deeper examination revealed a conference coordinator who did not want a training program on wellness; had asked to present her own topic; felt outside trainers were a personal affront to her own skills as an internal trainer, and basically wanted to prove that such a workshop would fail.

If you are looking for a word to describe all this, it's *sabotage*. And it's as unethical as it gets!

Examples of the same principle pop up in many ways in organizations and need to be exposed and stopped whenever and however they appear.

I could go on with my discussion of subtle unethical behaviors in organizations, but would probably need another 10 pages to do so. Let me instead simply list some other categories I have run across in my work as a consultant to groups in trouble:

- Pitting one person against another.
- Working to control personal turf at any cost.
- Withholding needed support.
- Incongruence between words and actions.
- Holding others accountable for unexpressed expectations.
- Passing judgments on personalities that have no bearing on the work.
- Black-mailing people personally (i.e.: "If you are really my friend, you'll do this.")
- Stealing work time for personal use.
- Misrepresenting what has or can be done.

- Score-keeping.
- Divulging confidential information.
- Falsifying reports.
- Accepting gifts or favors in exchange for preferential favors.
- Calling in sick when quite well.
- Concealing errors.
- Ignoring agency rules.

What we do both blatantly and subtly in the area of ethical behavior is the basis for our reputation personally and organizationally.

As people consider ethics more and more in this decade and beyond, we must see our most subtle actions as part of the potential appeal to others who seek to affiliate or collaborate with us.

No effort is too insignificant to be made ethically correct.

CODES OF ETHICS

Every agency, and in fact, every department, should have a code of ethics.

I urge you to make time for a retreat or quiet, un-interruptable setting, to brainstorm with interested parties those issues which need to be set down in writing as a code of ethical behavior. Address what can be done and what can't. List legal issues (tap an expert for this) and those broad codes which may impact you.

The Association for Volunteer Administration has a code of ethics statement for professionals in the field; the National Society of Fund Raising Executives has a code of ethics, etc. etc. Find any that apply to you and your organization, and discuss them with peers as you are putting your own code of ethics together.

Be specific in places and broad-based in others. Identify areas where ethical questions arise and discuss appropriate responses. Discuss and debate tough calls. Identify any areas where you cannot agree or need further assistance in charting the best course.

However you do it, however long it takes, no matter how complex it gets, keep it fair and practical, and DO IT! Keep wording simple and clear; avoid ambiguity; make it practical; align it with your mission and be ready and willing to change it if the need arises.

In addition to this frontal attack on unethical behavior, a more subtle but incredibly important part of setting and enforcing a code of ethics is the opportunity the volunteer program executive has to act as a role model for ethical behavior. When first interviewing volunteer applicants, when orienting new people, when working with staff to integrate volunteers into their department, find ways to reiterate the high standards of your department and yourself personally. Then demonstrate those standards through your actions.

Your lead in showing others how to work successfully inside a code of ethics is the best advertisement for high ethical standards. Through the admiration of those around you, you will lead others to right behavior, and will demonstrate that a positive public perception is well-deserved.

PUBLIC PERCEPTION

Every major trend-watcher speaks to some variation on the theme of the importance of how the public perceives organizations and individuals. There is a growing demand for congruence between actions and statements, between mission and activities, between what someone does and what they say they do.

Information specialists will probably grow in numbers and have their job designs changed to accommodate the public's demand for insight into how groups and institutions are doing their job.

Hospitals are already feeling this scrutiny, and churches are not far behind.

As health care costs skyrocketed in the 1980s and 1990s, the public came to believe that hospitals were wealthy beyond reason. They carried this perception to their planning calendars and were not as quick to volunteer there, feeling that *"they have enough money to pay for workers"*, and to their checkbooks as they believed *"they have more than enough money already"*.

It was not just the public that was looking at hospital and health care facilities with a new eye; the IRS and local taxing bodies also began to look at the nonprofit (tax free) status of many of these institutions and wonder if they would not be a rich source of revenue if part of this status was dropped.

Many communities decided to check on whether or not the hospitals were living up to their community service obligation which afforded them their tax exempt status. How did they go about checking? You guessed it.....via their volunteers!

The first level of scrutiny came to the Board, as municipalities began to carefully audit several factors about the volunteers found there, and asked:

- Were Board members totally conversant with the mission of the hospital?

- Were they simply figure-heads or actively involved?

- Were they out in the community, finding out what the public needed from the hospital?

- Were they then returning to the Board meetings, reporting the community needs and then helping to design and oversee programs to match these needs?

- Were the Board members reporting progress to the community, explaining programs and why any specific requests had to be laid aside or denied?

- Were these same Board volunteers carefully monitoring staff as programs were carried out?

- Were they also insuring that the hospital was indeed living up to its' community service mandate?

Looking carefully at how Board members interact as a liaison between the health care facility and the community is becoming a measuring stick for the credibility needed for them to continue to enjoy their tax exempt status. It is also a way to monitor public perception as Board members report their community experiences as they carry the messages between the public and the institution.

It does not take a genius to see the next logical step: Examining the volunteer services departments for similar interaction and responsiveness to community needs!

It is also apparent that the churches are about to come under close examination for the same reasons. The city council of Oakland, CA. voted to rescind the tax exempt status of churches, taking the position that some of their activities were self-serving rather than community-serving. When an uproar was felt after the ruling, it was tabled for "future review and action". But don't be fooled, churches, especially the non-traditional ones, will shortly be subject to careful examination for legitimacy, ethical practices and disclosure of resources.

It will be critical in the future that organizations continually find ways to monitor public perception and measure responsiveness, not just for tax reasons, but for all the nuances of how people .... (potential volunteers, supporters, donors, etc.).....view the entity. It will be from this perception that people will base their decisions for interaction, thus effecting the work of the volunteer program executive deeply.

I would suggest that any organization ask for the assistance of several of the largest civic and service organizations in their community, such as the Woman's Club, PTAs, Rotary, etc., to help them monitor public perception. Annual surveys can then go to members to test how the residents of the community perceive the agency and its work. What is perceived as the mission of the agency? Is it a good place to volunteer? What kinds of things would volunteers do there? Is it a good place to give donations? How would they spend the money? etc. etc.

I would guess that there may be a whole new career for folks willing to take the time to help groups audit public perception, then come back to the group to suggest ways to change the perceptions that are damaging and enhance those that are helpful or positive. Going well beyond PR or "Spin- Doctoring", they will need to be conversant with all aspects of the agency, but especially the volunteer component as it serves as the most visible bridge to the community.

It may be that the most important person on the Board, who traditionally has been avoided at all costs before, may be the one who asks the most difficult questions, harps on issues that seem to him to have been unanswered, holds everyone's feet to the fire until problems are solved, and points out the most minute crack in any plans! As the 'yes-people' of old are replaced by the valued questioner of today's society, it may be that old 'fly in the ointment' Board member who rises to the greatest height of honor and appreciation for keeping everything honest and aligned with the mission.

CLEAR ACCOUNTING

There is no more careful scrutiny by the public than on how resources are allocated.

If you don't already do so, include a financial pie chart in any materials handed out to the public so that at a glance, and in the simplest of terms, people can see how you spend your dollars and where those dollars come from.

It was not until the President of a struggling airline opened the books to his employees that they truly understood why he had said no to higher wages. By assembling representatives from all phases of his operation and allowing them access to all financial records, he reversed a mis-perception by employees that the airline was concealing millions of dollars they could be enjoying in the way of higher wages and increased benefits.

The disclosure established a new relationship between management and labor which allowed the company to survive difficult times. Everyone had the same information, and a relationship of trust replaced one of adversarial entities; we-they thinking was turned into "us" and layers of misunderstanding, inappropriate perceptions and unfair conclusions were wiped away.

104

Remember in dealing with the issues of ethics and perception, that you are not just talking about external perceptions from outside your organization of what you are doing, but also the perceptions of those internally, who work based on what they perceive you to be. Help everyone involved to have the information they need to understand motives, behaviors, decisions and actions. Involve them in the decision-making process and the implementation of directives, so that they feel they have some control in matters.

Public perceptions, internally and externally, are critical to success. People must believe that they can trust the institution and the people who lead it, so that they feel safe in offering their support, their time and their resources in a legitimate, ethical setting.

WHEN MISTAKES ARE MADE

Address and correct them immediately.

Whether the public perception is correct or not, attack it head on!

Remember the Tylenol and Pepsi examples of the early 1990s? When Tylenol bottles were tampered with in the Chicago area, causing several deaths, Tylenol executives addressed the horror immediately, removing their product from shelves across the country, and sharing all information as the culprit was tracked. They took every step possible to restore confidence by the public in their product by re-designing the packaging to be tamper-proof (a new phrase in our vocabulary) and setting up a hot line for people to call to share their concerns.

When, several years later, there were a number of statements by Pepsi buyers that needles and syringes were found in cans of the popular beverage, Pepsi immediately began to work with law enforcement agencies across the country to discover the truth. They too set up a hot line for people to call and carefully examined the claims and canning procedures for flaws that would allow tampering.

When it was proved that the initial complaint was an honest

105

mistake (an elderly man picked up a can left by a diabetic relative, who had disposed of an insulin syringe in the half-full can, and thought it had just been opened) and the rest were copycat claims of people hoping for monetary compensation for "injury", they then took out full page ads in papers and began a TV campaign to reassure the public of their product safety.

In neither case did these companies try to bury the information, adopt a "it could never be!" attitude, deny public concern or accuse anyone of sabotage. Their focus was what was best for the public safety and how they could keep the public informed as intense investigations went along.

Their example has hopefully set the standard for any group who experiences a real or perceived misstep in the future:

- Admit the problem.
- Investigate it openly and honestly, without preconceptions or defensiveness.
- Keep the public informed.
- Do everything possible to restore public confidence.
- Demonstrate ethical behavior.

What a wonderful world it would be if every person and organization adopted this policy of disclosure and ethics so that little problems could remain little and big problems could be avoided rather than further magnified by people denying they exist!

The Volunteer Program Executive must lead the way in assessing every action, service and effort of the organization to insure the highest standards of ethical practice, and to help the public obtain all the information it needs to be assured of this standard.

Chapter 7

BUILDING COMMUNITY:
Focus on Organization, Capacity & Networking

"Where community exists it confers upon its members identity, a sense of belonging, a measure of security. Individuals acquire a sense of self partly from their continuous relationships to others, and from the culture of their native place.   The ideas of justice and compassion are nurtured in communities."

...John Gardner, *"Building Community"*

"The community that is needed in society has to be based on commitment and compassion rather than being imposed by proximity and isolation."

......Peter Drucker, *"Post Capitalist Society"*

In our newly transformed world we will need to adapt to new patterns of thinking and working, creating communities within and around our organizations, private lives and initiatives.

The Lone Ranger isolation that prompted narrowed vision, territorial squabbles along with incredible leader-burnout and follower-disgust will be forced to evaporate in the face of increased access to information, shrinking resources and the need for answers to life or death questions.

ORGANIZATIONS

We will, I believe, expand our definition of 'organization' to bring new life to Peter Drucker's definition:

> *"An organization is a human group, composed of specialists working together on a common task. It is always specialized. It is defined by its task."*

> *"Post Capitalist Society"* Drucker

As we venture into a new century, we will find shifts in how our current organizations define themselves and organize new "partnering" arrangements around common concerns.

Who are You? Why are You? Where are You Going?....

Current organizations in volunteer-related work will need to continually do a self-assessment to answer these three questions:

1. **Who Are You?** Who is your constituency? What binds them together? What commonalties exist?

2. **Why Are You?** Why have you come together? What do you want to accomplish? What justifies the effort it takes to stay together? What's your purpose?

3. **Where Are You Going?** What's your mission? What actions are you taking to attain your mission? What do you envision as success?

For several years authors such as Tom Peters and Robert Waterman (*"In Search of Excellence"*, etc.) have been talking more and more strongly about the payoffs that come to those organizations which are "mission-driven".

For years I have harped on the same theme by asking training audiences to tell me what business they are in.

Just as Peters and Waterman discovered through their research on characteristics of excellence in business, and I in my simple questioning, the most outstanding groups knew precisely what their mission was...others, sadly in the majority, did not.

I once was called into the headquarters of one of the top national charities.

They had sent me a box (literally) of annual reports, newsletters, audits, statistics and about 6 consultant's "conclusions" to help me understand their complex organization before I visited their headquarters.

Their request of me was that I uncover what was causing so much staff unrest, burnout, turnover, and even shrinking donor dollars. They were also concerned about an obvious lack of creative thinking throughout the organization.

I glanced over a few departmental final reports, looked at the group's history and reviewed their financial statement. With a growing suspicion tucked away in my "hmmmmm" file, I headed for NY and a face-to-face meeting with the CEO and 10 department heads.

After the necessary introductions and pleasantries and a speech by the CEO indicating his willingness to help me "get to the root of our problems", he turned the meeting over to me.

With some trepidation and a quick glance to reassure myself that I had a return airline ticket to home and safety, I asked them to write down, without consultation with anyone else, what business they were in and what they were trying to do as an organization.

I ignored the exasperated body language from the assemblage (the "Oh no, another touchy-feely consultant" reaction) and asked them to hand me their written answers.

As the responses came in to me, I glanced at what was written and confirmed my previous suspicions. To also uncover some valuable information on relationships, I then read the CEO's answer which garbled on about how the organization was designed to provide the most efficient and effective model among health-related charities and to deliver services in a cost effective manner.

I read his statement with no comment and hoped my facial expression was neutral enough to hide my real desire to chuckle!

The room was quiet for a few seconds, then began a cacophony of 10 grown men trying to out-garble each other as they verbalized their complete agreement with the CEO. You could sense in a few a desperate hope that I wouldn't read their own written responses as they amended what they'd said to align it with the CEOs.

At this point I rechecked my plane ticket, made sure I knew where the EXIT was, and blithely said, "No need to try to rewrite your original answers to look like your bosses, no one in the room produced the right answer for the organization."

Stunned silence.

Everyone exchanged eye checks with the CEO to see how he was going to respond. Each began to prepare for defensiveness.

I then asked a volunteer I had just met in the outer office (she was preparing a mailing) to step into the Board Room (a first for her I suspected) to answer a question. I was prepared for any answer but prayed for the correct one.

She didn't let me down.

"Uhh....well, it's to help kids with (the disease) and their families, I'd say."

And she was right.

Before 11 grown men became unglued trying to tell me that that was "too simple" or "too obvious" or "what I meant", I let them off the hook by telling them I'd worked with dozens of groups such as theirs and rarely did any executives give such a simple, direct answer.

Time and again, as people work in their organizations the overwhelming focus becomes their own personal assignment, and they frame everything that surrounds them, even the total organization's MISSION, by that perspective.

Thus, CEOs see the Mission as working to be organizationally sound......

Directors of Development see it as gathering money.....

Directors of Volunteers see it as successfully recruiting volunteers to do work....

Directors of Programs see it as efficiently and effectively functioning.....

Directors of PR see it as shedding light and telling the story as widely as possible....

Directors of Personnel see it as acquiring enough people to do the work....

and on and on.

Now, before you begin to defend all those perspectives let me say that in their own settings or departments they are correct, as they are describing the goal of their part of the puzzle of the overall organization.

Think back to the first part of Drucker's definition: *"An organization is a human group, composed of specialists..."* What department directors typically do is define the entire organization from the point of view of their specialty so that the CEO feels justified in concentrating on his or her organizing specialty, and each department head in turn focuses on their specific expertise and assignment.

Within the confines of their job description they are correct about their specialty, but typically, they end the description of their role at that point, leaving out the rest of Drucker's definition that extends beyond their department......

Megatrends & Volunteerism

*"...working together on a **common task**. An organization is always specialized. It is defined by its task."*

Sadly, many organizations have not really defined their task, or once having done so, never revisit it to check it against the reality of the times or its relevancy to changing needs.

One of the greatest demands from the general public and potential volunteers is that organizations must be relevant, efficient and focused like a laser on their mission. As time and energy supplies shrink for people juggling a thousand demands, they must feel that whatever they offer an organization is worth the price they are going to pay to share their valuable time and energy.

For organizations to respond to this increasing demand they will have to KNOW WHAT BUSINESS THEY ARE IN AND WHAT THEIR MISSION IS! It is from this starting point, this basic foundation, that organizations build community.

They will then be monitored by the public at large and the volunteers specifically to insure that every action they take, every resource they allocate is measured against this mission....

☞ Does this project contribute to the mission?

☞ Is this action in line with the spirit of the mission?

☞ Will this action bring us closer to our mission?

☞ Can these people support and commit to our mission?

☞ Do our materials reflect our mission?

and harder questions even...

☞ Is our mission relevant to our times?

☞ Can some other group serve our mission more effectively?

☞ Is there a better way to achieve our mission?

112

Building Community

 Are there more appropriate people who can attain our mission?

When groups are mission-driven; when every level in the organization is aware of and personally committed to the mission; when the mission is used as a measuring tool for everything and everyone.....then it truly becomes _"a human group, working together on a common task."_

When the mission becomes a dynamic, vital, clear force within a group, the visual image often changes from one of individuals each playing a strong but different tune in frequent discord and occasional, random blending, to one of masterful orchestration and harmony between different instruments playing the same symphony.

The focus becomes the combined efforts to achieve a single, stated goal. It becomes a community of people working together toward a vision of something better.

The New York group had to refocus on the simple goal of helping children and their families with a specific, deadly disease. In so doing they began to emerge from the confusion and demands caused by people going off in different directions, giving mixed signals to those who wished to follow. Further discussions with various departments and all levels of workers uncovered some elementary confusion as to what the group's mission really was....Research? Fund raising? Cure of the disease? Public awareness? Helping victims?

No wonder people burned out, gave up and left. No wonder work seemed harder, tempers flared, departments fought among themselves, people felt betrayed....very few were heading toward the same definition of success.

If organizations are to survive into the 21st century, they must return to their roots, uncover them for all to see and then measure their efforts against those roots, rejecting the temptation of trying to be all things to all people.

A major "Megatrend" for our times is the call to define Mission and then stick to it! And the successful attainment of that mission-driven focus sets the stage for the community that is so obviously longed for in society today.....a safe place to gather, to work together, share life and be supportive to one another.

RESISTING TYRANNICAL PRESSURE:
The Founder Syndrome

For organizations to be seen as caring communities that are attractive to people, they will need to take a strong stance as individuals attempt to influence their actions. Across America a swelling cry is beginning to take shape:

Arrogance is OUT!   Accountability is IN!

Think back to the tides that have turned as once influential people, used to always having their way, have been punished for an arrogant attitude of, "I am the Ruler, All must Obey!": TV Evangelists, junk-bond kings, CEOs of major private and nonprofit corporations, a hotel "Queen", sports stars & champions, politicians, cult leaders, etc. Every one of them thought of themselves as somehow above the rules, exempt from the laws of accountability and responsibility all the rest of us must obey, and entitled to special privileges.

Every trend-watcher notes that the mood in America has turned against such people who have been caught up in their own web of self-proclaimed Messiahood (in my book on wellness, "How To Take Care of You", I talk about people who get so caught up in their own celebrity that they become silly enough to believe their own press clippings!...Same affliction.).

 Each of the people alluded to above paid a terrible price for believing that they were somehow above the rules. Jail terms, banishment from the national scene, bankruptcy, disgrace, job loss and even death.....with their arrogance going up in flames as they belligerently defended their positions and rationalized their actions.

Each had come to believe that what they said or commanded be done would and must be obeyed. Peter Drucker warns us loudly of being caught up in the grasp of such tyrants who demand obedience and lead groups into dysfunction as members attempt to either obey short-sighted orders or avoid confrontation by ignoring the demands. He states, bluntly: *"Organizations must resist the pressure of the tyranny of the small minority."*

In a healthy community, no one can be a tyrant, no matter how they cover their tyranny with sweet smiles, proclamations of caring and love or great good works.

In many groups, this issue becomes a painful one which I have dubbed the "Founder Syndrome" and marks a difficult part of the path to organizational maturity. Healthy communities must be mature and provide a climate that is fair, safe and empowering. Trust must exist as the lubricant for the engine of activity in any size group....a trust strong enough to tolerate differences and reject a need for total control.

> *"Trust is making oneself vulnerable to others whose subsequent behavior we cannot control*
> ....J.M. Kouzes, B.Z. Posner,
> "The Leadership Challenge"

> *"A lack of trust inhibits flow of information, sharing of resources, and reciprocity of influence. It usually leads to deteriorating problem solving, and lack of detection of inappropriate solutions and underlying problems."*
>
> ...Catherine Sweeney, Ph.D..,
> "Teamwork & Collaboration in Volunteer Groups.

MILEPOSTS OF DEVELOPMENT

Frequently, as an organization grows it marks several mileposts of maturation....

1. **Birth** because of a charismatic leader who sees a need, plots a course of action and recruits others to join them in making it happen.

2. **Infancy,** where systems and actions are put together out of necessity and often with much trial and error to reach the goal

115

of the group. New people are added to the core group around the founder because they share the vision proclaimed by them and have specific expertise to lend to the effort.

3. **Adolescence**, where systems and actions are formalized and standardized for the good of the organization itself, and in an effort to reach goals in an efficient manner. More specialists are added to run the group and others are recruited as auxiliary supporters who contribute money, resources, goods and services. A more formalized governing body takes shape which responds to the best interests of the mission and in response to the collective voices of the supporters and clients.

4. **Young adulthood,** when the above constituency begins to demand specific service needs, programs or a greater voice in determining how things are done within and by the organization.

It is frequently at stage 3 or 4, when these new voices begin to speak of change, that the Founder Syndrome can rear its ugly head.

Someone suggests a change in the way things have been done since the founder first did it "in the beginning", and suddenly you find yourself in the middle of WW III!

Many groups have been shocked to see their benevolent, wise, caring, visionary suddenly turning into Atilla the Hun or Ma Barker when change is suggested. They have absolutely no clue as to why the founder has become a tyrant and are at a loss to know what to do to handle the situation.

What they are dealing with is what a Japanese Suicideologist, Dr. Inamura, has labeled the "Theory of Significance". In short it states that whenever a person feels his or her significance is going to be diminished, they will fight to the death to protect it. Most sadly, when people feel their significance is over, some will take their own life. (His research points to this sense of loss of significance in a great number of people who did indeed commit suicide.)

The problem is that for many years the typical founder or major leader of a group, movement or effort, has poured all their energies and resources into furthering the effort, rightly gaining followers who not only helped carry out necessary work, but were totally grateful...sometimes even worshipful....of the founder and their vision.

The founder made decisions and pronouncements that others followed and which brought about success and growth. In the process the leader became used to being listened to, agreed with, obeyed and seen as correct in their judgments. Subtly, within the founder, a switch has occurred from focus on the action to focus on the being; from doing the right thing to being right; from choosing wisely to feeling they alone know the "one correct way" to do something.

Basically, it is a confusion between worth and work.....a foggy overlap that convinces a person that what they DO is who they ARE. In a world before the women's movement of the 60s and 70s this was thought to be a male affliction, but through progress (?), it has equally become a problem for women who see themselves as significant only through their work rather than as a whole, rounded personality.

Thus, the founder of an organization which feeds starving children is horrified when he suggests in a speech that the group will begin a drug-rehabilitation program and the Board says, "No, that is not our mission, we will not do that" and the founder tries to gather forces to remove the Board members.

He is not used to having anyone say "no" to him; he sees the organization as "his".

A business tycoon decides she is above the rules and does not have to pay taxes "like all the little people" and a court says, "no, you are not exempt" and she goes off to jail totally dumfounded and crying "foul!".

She is not used to having her decisions challenged.

A religious icon is accused by followers of mishandling funds and reneging on promises of life-long vacation sites and he goes to jail professing his innocence amid further revelations of personal misconduct.

He was convinced that his work on behalf of God gave him the "right" to do as he pleased.

Politicians saw themselves as untouchable and therefore able to act in ways that clearly broke laws, but then were astonished to hear the American people or their peers saying, "No, you are just as accountable to the law of the land as any citizen" and therefore driven from office by voters or forced to resign in disgrace.

They were used to doing as they pleased.

A CEO builds an organization from the ground up to become an international force but is shocked when his resignation is forced after years of discontent in the ranks which boils over into internal investigations that show misuse of money, power and influence.

He believed what he took was "owed" him by right of having devoted his life to the organization.

It is the same in groups of any size.

A church Pastor is shocked to have his edict rejected and starts such a war within the congregation that it is split in half, each side going their own way; a charity announces that its founder will no longer be the spokesperson for the group and she leaves to form a new group that she can control, causing chaos in the original organization; a leader insists an organization to which they belong go in one direction but they choose another and the leader is bewildered, wounded and works desperately to win others to their "side", only to find a widening gap between themselves, the organization and its direction.

None of the above examples are from my imagination; all are actual cases of various degrees of tyranny within communities and are the Founder Syndrome in action.

When groups resist such tyranny, two things result:

1. **The organization matures** and sets itself on a course of fair, democratic decision-making that measures actions against the mission of the organization rather than the mindset of one or a few individuals. (This obviously assumes that one tyrant has

not been replaced by another or, worse yet, an organized group of tyrants!)

2. **New people are attracted** to the organization as they see it as a community that offers a collaborative, trust-worthy climate in which people can thrive.

The trend toward community so evidenced in the words of almost every author I consulted in writing this book is one of the strongest at work at the end of the 20th century. One of the most notable mistakes any group might make is allowing the Founder Syndrome to get a toe hold, as it will do more to damage the organization than almost any other factor.

What To Do If The "Founder Syndrome" Is Already At Work?

It is amazing to talk about this syndrome with my consulting or training clients and see the light bulbs go off in people's eyes as they identify atypical behavior from a founder or leader in their program! They tell me that they could never figure out what had turned their normally benign, friendly and loving founder into a raging, wounded bear, leaving admirers bewildered and "opposing" organizational leaders bloodied.

Once knowing what they were up against, however, they knew better how to de-escalate the problem and avoid further blood shed.

I share here what many groups have done to minimize this blood-letting that can bring the largest organization to a stand-still, cause good people to go elsewhere rather than fight, and erode public confidence:

1. Most groups can reduce the resistance from founders by dramatically **insuring that they get credit** for their contributions. Research details of the founder/leader's contributions if you are not familiar with them directly. Look at programs or initiatives they first introduced.

2. **Understand their motivational base...** David McClelland's work on personal motivational categories helps here. Determine whether they are an Affiliator, Achiever or Power person. Remember that everyone is all three, but one dominates. In

Founder Syndrome cases it's usually a matter of being in a power phase and the need to personally control the group and its actions. Beyond their phase, you will need to understand their primary or base motivation and handle them accordingly, tailoring recognition and approaches differently. Affiliators want recognition in people-related ways; Achievers want recognition in factual or systemic ways; Power people want recognition in terms of influence and impact ways.

3. **Design appropriate recognition** and validation of them AS AN INDIVIDUAL who has contributed greatly to the growth and development of the group, program or field. Be careful to be specific. You might consider naming a facility, award or program for them to continually recognize their contribution.

4. **Show how their contribution provided the foundation** or link that made subsequent growth possible. Here is where you show how what they did enabled the effort you are now trying to institute, to be possible. Hopefully this makes them see themselves as a critically important part of dynamic growth rather than an isolated contributor of yesteryear.

5. **Bring them into planning of efforts** that do indeed build on their contributions, garnering the wisdom and perspective they have. Do this as long as they offer honest feedback untainted by any need to shoot down new ideas in order to preserve their own status. Listen to what they have to say positively. Be watchful for sabotage but do not assume it will arise.

Should they revert to the old resistance motives of feeling personally threatened, REMOVE THEM FROM THE PLANNING LOOP to avoid contamination and energy drain. If this sounds harsh, it is, but remember the steps for successful organizations which begin with "eliminate that which does not work; remove impediments to growth and success".

And one general warning should you encounter the Founder Syndrome and need to take steps to reassure the person about their significance:

NEVER RECOGNIZE ANYONE INSINCERELY!

Insincerity comes across, accurately, as manipulation, condescension and degradation. False praise reminds me of vanilla flavoring: smells great but tastes bitter!

And three last bits of advice on the Founder Syndrome and the healthy community you are trying to build:

1. When you've survived such a Founder battle, forgive the founder and move on.

2. Someday YOU'LL probably hear your program or organization suggest changes to things YOU initiated. It will then be your opportunity to step aside gracefully and refuse to be afflicted with the Founder Syndrome.

3. Do not assume that all founders or leaders will cause this problem of resisting change..actually most don't become an impediment to growth, but instead, take on the role of proud parent, seeing what they created take on a whole new identity by finding new ways to be effective and grow into maturity. In the field of volunteerism we have a long list of such people, headed by Brian O'Connell, who wisely guided Independent Sector and for all of his years of leading and mentoring that fine group, never once fell victim to the arrogance that has defeated others.

Other examples exist, but by going on with specific names, I would be sure to leave out others, so, with my belief that less is better, I'll simply tip my hat to Brian and the other thousands of his character who have lead by example rather than dictate.

DIVERSITY: Different Perspectives on the Same Topic

It is interesting to note that the major writers of trends....Drucker, Aburdene, Naisbitt, Popcorn, Peters, etc.........see diversity from different perspectives, though all agree that diversity is a major factor that will influence what we do and how we act as individuals and organizations.

Megatrends & Volunteerism

As I have mentioned several other times in this book in different contexts, Peter Drucker is speaking out about 'tribalism', which he sees as divisive because it focuses on what is different between people rather than what unifies them. He offers example after example of peoples such as those in Eastern Europe who are warring over sometimes ancient conflicts of original tribes.

He explains the trend as a desire to find roots and to be part of a community because bigness no longer confers much advantage. People need to define themselves, their identify and mission in terms that can be understood.

The other writers speak of diversity as a positive force that will bring varied perspectives to efforts and forge new alliances that are more in touch with grassroots needs.

Somewhere between these two perspectives is, I believe, the truth regarding diversity......Many groups will struggle to bring diversity into their ranks, making it stronger by so doing. We must, however be mindful of the negative potential of focusing only on differences, and instead, focus on the melding of diverse people to a common goal.

In this process of melding, directors of volunteer programs will need to model an openness to differences and a pattern of concentrating on commonalties rather than those differences which have nothing to do with the work required. In other words:

"If it doesn't matter, don't let it matter!"

If the goal is to feed homeless people in a shelter and a volunteer has a speech impairment, it doesn't matter.

If the goal is to help clean up the environment by clearing trash from a river bank and a volunteer appears in long, unkempt hair and ragged clothing, it doesn't matter.

If the goal is to cuddle and comfort babies dying of aids and the volunteer is visually impaired, it doesn't matter.

If, on the other hand, the long-haired volunteer wished to serve food or the person visually impaired wanted to clear trash, these factors would indeed matter, though their "differences" could be worked around creatively to include them in serving.

In a healthy community, there are diverse people with different capabilities, challenges and backgrounds. If the volunteer administrator can keep their eye on melding these diversities into a collection of different people working toward a **common** goal, they have taken a giant step toward community.

BUILDING COMMUNITY IN OUR VOLUNTEER PROGRAMS

As we see the need for community expressed in various examples around us, we need to find ways to bring a sense of community to our volunteer programs.

In so doing we must keep in mind that a major trend that will influence volunteers attraction and tenure will be that of **safety**....feeling safe from failure, harm or stress.

John Gardner, in *Building Community,* speaks to the characteristics a sound society provides individuals. I believe these same characteristics apply to the sound community volunteer program executives will need to offer individuals in their agencies and organizations:

1. **Nurture in infancy:** providing strong orientation and training as the volunteers first come to work within the program; answering questions and concerns honestly; paying directed attention to individuals as they first interact with systems, clients and fellow workers; establishing trust.

2. **Secure environment in which to mature:** strengthening the trust relationship through relational management; providing increasing information as skills develop; offering empowering supervision appropriate to the individual and tasks at hand; involving participants in decisions which affect them.

3. **Framework of meaning:** a clear articulation of the mission of the organization; the mission used as a standard against which all actions are measured; everyone familiar with the vision of the organization as it attains the mission; systems, activities and resource allocations all mission-driven.

123

4. **Sense of identity and belonging:** understanding where an individual "fits" as a volunteer in the total picture of the program or organization; honestly-earned sense of how important their contributions are to the work being done and the character of the program; appreciation for how the community embraces both volunteers and paid staff working together to serve clients or consumers; seeing the vision of the effort and where it impacts the greater communities to which it belongs (the general population, the field of voluntary community service, the sub-culture it represents such as health care, arts, recreation, religion, etc.)

5. **Reward & recognition for accomplishment:** offering appropriate appreciation for what the volunteers and paid staff partners have contributed; individualizing rewards in accordance with the specific efforts, needs, preferences and motivations of the workers; understanding that recognition is 'user-oriented'; giving recognition continually and at the time of the contribution; avoiding a score-keeping mentality that only recognizes the people with the most hours, biggest contribution, longest service etc.; understanding that recognition is as meaningful when it is informal (friendly "hello" each day, reserved place to park, personalized coffee cup, birthday card, etc.) as it is when it is more formal (annual banquet, certificate, etc.).

Gardner suggests that when people sense the fairness, safety, and camaraderie of the community spirit, they give back to it:

    1. Allegiance to the vision; feeling a moral responsibility to the mission.
    2. Commitment to the community.
    3. Positive actions by doing good work.

Certainly all of those results are exactly what CEOs and volunteer program executives are looking for as paid and non-paid staff work together within the framework of programs to serve clients.

They are seeking a sense of community which others will recognize, hopefully influencing those others to become part of the work for a long period of time. A community that cares, nurtures, empowers success and initiates recognition, and that can carry us safely into the 21st century.

BUILDING ON CAPACITY

There is a growing trend that is shifting from a focus on incapacity to one of a focus on capacity; emphasis on the positive rather than the negative.

This trend will help shape volunteer programs and entrepreneurial activities for many years to come as it helps leaders wishing to impact issues to assess where they are, determine what resources they have to build on and then map out ways to accomplish their goal.

In the past, groups have tended to audit their efforts based on what *incapacities* can be spotted, although now we see many of them shifting toward looking at *capacities* or strengths first. This shift in attitude and perspective influences greatly the atmosphere and character of any community.

If you have ever been part of a group whose leaders constantly play the "ain't-it-awful" game, you know how depressing it can be. Such an attitude can impart a sense of uselessness in expending energies. A "why try?" response prevails as deficiencies are emphasized to such a degree that it seems hopeless to even attempt to rectify them.

In the next ten years I believe we will see an increased focus on capacity and an appreciation for people who can find creative ways to recognize and build on strengths.

Healthy communities of workers will embrace a simple, four step method I first introduced in my book on marketing as I described how to get who and what you might need:

   1. What do you HAVE?
        2. What do you NEED?
        3. Who HAS what you need?
        4. How do you GET what you need?

In working with groups, I find that usually they begin their process of development with question number two, "What do we NEED?", thereby automatically focusing on deficiencies. Instead the first step needs to be on what we HAVE.....the equivalent of saying,

"Before I write a check, I had better know what money I have in the bank", or, "Before I begin to build my house, I had better know what tools and materials I have to use".

In a capacity-focused organizational community, leaders will need to first look around to see what strengths, resources and capabilities they have to lend to the challenges of step number two, the identification of needs.

There are several entities that assist groups doing capacity-audits or mapping so that they can first identify strengths and second, to feel good about what they have. It is not unusual for people to overlook capacities, therefore it might be helpful to have an outsider help in this capacity-mapping.

This first assessment will also uncover some needs that might otherwise have been left in the dark, thereby offering more solid information on which to build and timeline activities.

The volunteer administrators of the future will need to have the ability and attitude to plan positively, with their focus on capacities rather than incapacities. What CAN we do will be the starting point rather than what we can NOT do.

Once those capacities are mapped, it will become the role of the volunteer service executives to continually add to the list so that growth and strength can be identified and these resources can stand ready for all future planning as foundations for success.

A secondary role for the volunteer administrator will be to continually help others "connect the dots" between resources and needs, helping people see how the strengths inherent in the community can be put to use to meet identified needs.

After determining resources and needs, the volunteer administrator can then decide who might be able to supply the needs and how best to establish a 'win-win' exchange between the two entities. For the relationship to be successful, it is critical that all parties feel they have received a fair exchange of value for value. In the four step marketing process, this attitude of caring about what the other party gets out of the relationship, MUST underline all negotiations.

126

BUILDING NETWORKS

In the focus on community, it is important to see the natural expansion of multiple communities as networks, connected in a 'super-community' manner which can draw on the capacities and strengths of all parties as they work toward common visions.

Networking is simply a manifestation of the trend toward collaboration, coordination and cooperation, three driving forces that have been shaping our corporations, organizations, communities and institutions for several years.

In networks, the same principles apply as in communities: a clear vision and purpose for coming together; action to attain the vision; a belief that combined strengths can accomplish the goal.

And as in communities, the key ingredient to success in networks is trust.....the capacity to assume the positive, relinquish need for total control, believe in the good faith and works of others and remain flexible.

A healthy network or collaborative effort is mature, never whines, and refuses to waste energy blaming. Road blocks are seen as opportunities for bridges, as problems are for solutions. It is never petty, shares information and does not play games.

Within collaborative networks, there is an assumption of excellence and good intention. It does not get hung up on rules and structures, but works by common sense toward goals and is willing to shift course if a clearer path becomes available.

Such networks are simply larger examples of "Leadershift", so that those assembled around an issue each bring to the effort a needed perspective or strength, and when these are paramount to the work, they take on the leadership role which shifts to recognize their contribution.

In networks, as in communities, there is an ultimately responsible leader, who, like the orchestra conductor, makes sure everyone is working together toward the common goal. This person hopefully is wise enough to let everyone involved do what they do best, and therefore steps aside to allow them the joy of lending their strength to the overall effort.

Megatrends & Volunteerism

The wise volunteer program executive is constantly looking for network partners, so that they can tap the resources already out there, and avoid reinventing the wheel. They seek partnering arrangements rather than now-and-forever partnerships, so that they can move in and out of networks as concerns shift.

Locally they often seek a network for themselves in the form of DOVIAs (local support groups of Directors Of Volunteers In Agencies). They also seek wider network communities such as the Association for Volunteer Administration, Points of Light Foundation, National Society of Fund Raising Executives, Independent Sector, American Society of Directors of Volunteer Services or other communities specifically tailored to their needs.

Within their population area, they seek or create networks with like-minded groups or people who then jointly address problems or challenges; in their neighborhoods they join with friends and acquaintances to make where they live a better or safer place.

Networks simply are a way for groups and individuals to join hands in shared efforts, bringing strength to one another and the vision they have for the world they share.

In the cry for community, they are the life-blood for a better tomorrow.

> **"The communities we build today may eventually be eroded or torn apart by the crosscurrents of contemporary life. Then we rebuild. We can't know all the forms community will take, but we know the values and the kinds of supporting structures we want to preserve. We are a community-building species. We might become remarkably ingenious at creating new forms of community for a swiftly changing world."**
>
> ....John Gardner, *Building Community*

Chapter 8

EXPANDED EXPERTISE

"Good anticipation is the result of good strategic exploration....and in time of turbulence the ability to anticipate dramatically enhances your chances of success."
...Joel Arthur Barker, "Future Edge"

"Fear of knowing is very deeply a fear of doing."
..Abraham Maslow.

The volunteer coordinator of the next century will have to command a broader and broader range of expertise to be able to meet the challenges of leading volunteer efforts within organizations. Far deeper than simply knowing how to plan, organize, staff, direct, control and reward, the Volunteer Program Executive will have to move far beyond these basic functions of management to embrace techniques and strategies that are both complex and interdependent

Armed with knowledge, including how we access special expertise, the volunteer program leader will have to hone skills of communication, climate, technical and sensitivity issues and a dozen more!

Rather than just managing volunteers, she will need to empower the entire organization around her to be the best they can be.......no small challenge, even for those in our profession used to Super-human efforts!

FROM MANAGERS TO INFORMATION EXPERTS

Peter Drucker, in his 1993 book, "Post Capitalist Society", points out the shift in definitions of managers from the 1950 version that said a manager.....

"is responsible for the performance of people"....

to the early 1990's definition of a manager being one who.....

"is responsible for the application and performance of knowledge."

This shift means that we see knowledge as the essential resource that when applied effectively, can enable us to obtain people, support, capital and things, all necessary ingredients in goal-attainment.

By gathering, assessing and applying information, we will be able to recruit, integrate, support, retain and recognize volunteers and paid staff as they work together toward the missions of our agencies.

This means that volunteer administrators will need to manage their time to include the too-often-put-off reading of new materials and attendance at carefully selected, pertinent seminars and workshops. This will require some creative juggling of work loads as demands pull in a multitude of directions.

Directors of volunteers will have to restructure their time and energy allotment to include the gathering of information and to refuse to allow this gathering to be on the bottom of their priority list.

Too frequently I've spoken with volunteer program executives who have burned out from work over-load. When I ask what they feel like (feelings are facts!), I usually hear that they can no longer cope with the constant drain on their energies as people around and above them demand more and more from them.

It will be essential for volunteer program executives to restructure their time in order to gather and share information while shifting from the managing of *volunteers* to the management of *systems* that empower goal attainment.

130

Expanded Expertise

It will not be easy for many such volunteer managers to change from their normal routine of working directly with volunteers to the management of systems and the role of information-conduit, but time and work load will force the metamorphous. The effective volunteer program executive of the 21st century will need to gather information and be able to sort it for pertinence, then give it to those who need it in easy-to-understand form.

Information will be the currency of tomorrow.

THE VOLUNTEER PROGRAM EXECUTIVE AS KNOWLEDGE-SHARER

Volunteer administrators will have to constantly be an agent for others as they help to transfer knowledge from the information source to the information user.

To do this effectively, they will have to understand and apply techniques of communication which embrace:

1. User-friendly presentation.

2. Word-economy.

3. Translation to user's language.

4. Application examples.

5. Appropriate adult-learning principles.

User-friendliness: To transfer knowledge to those who must use it, the presentation of the information must be in a format that encourages learning. Too often good information stumbles over its form of delivery.....

☞ Regulations are written in lengthy and complex wording that looks so formidable, few even try to read it.

☞ Ideas are presented in scatter-gun fashion rather than a logical, step-by-step format, causing listeners to become totally confused.

☞ Too much information is given, overwhelming people with things that don't even apply to them.

☞ Pages of information are jammed so full of type that the reader is discouraged from being able to get through it, let alone find the answers to their basic questions of, "what should I do?" and "what do I need to know?"

Word Economy: Lincoln's Gettysburg address is a masterful example of word economy, as the vast majority of words where one-syllable and had five letters or less. The whole speech took only a few minutes (compared to a two hour-long speech that preceded his address!) yet it conveyed a vision that shaped the entire course of reconstruction and the healing of a nation.

The rule of thumb to keep in mind therefore, when communicating information so that others may respond, is:

"Never use quarter words when nickel ones will do."

Enough said.

Translation: Beyond the obvious use of the actual language of workers when communicating with non-English-speaking people, we will have to find ways to communicate with others in speech and examples familiar to their experience.

In other words: Avoid Ph.D. language when trying to communicate with high schoolers; don't give examples of programs based in white suburbia to people of color living in urban public housing or farmers in small rural communities; avoid 'hip' phrases used by MTV fans when talking to older retirees.

Get to know the individuals and groups you will address so well that you can 'speak their language' and use appropriate words, examples and contexts to help them be comfortable with the information you are sharing. Keep in mind that the goal is to transfer information so that the receiver will be able to **USE** it.

Application Examples: As new information must be shared, identify or create examples of how the information can be put to use. Do not assume that everyone understands the concept you might be sharing and be able to translate it into action.

Learn to build word-pictures of actions so that others can see them clearly.

Adult Learning: Because most volunteer directors work with adults, it is vital that they build a personal expertise in adult learning principles. Even if you work with youth volunteers, these same principles have relevance.

In my book, *The Great Trainer's Guide: How To Train (almost) Anyone to Do (almost) Anything,* I've shared over 170 pages on the topic of adult learning that has no place in this work. Let me summarize the key points here which volunteer leaders will need to understand regarding how adults learn:

1. They have more experience and like to apply it to learning.
2. They are ready to learn ...they are there by choice.
3. They want the information now! Cut to the chase!
4. They want learning to be practical. Forget pie-in-the-sky.
5. They have a clearer self-concept than children and can usually tell you what they need to know.

Adults usually learn in one of three ways: by *hearing* information, by *seeing* it, or by *practicing* it. This knowledge should help in planning training so that it includes lecture, visuals and hands-on experiences.

In this, the Information Age, those who work to direct volunteer energies will have to develop skills of expert-communicator, so that knowledge can be put to use to achieve the mission of service organizations.

THE VOLUNTEER PROGRAM EXECUTIVE
AS TREND-WATCHER

Our communication expertise must be matched with an ability to seek out and translate demographic and trend data from various sources.

It will not be enough to simply pour over Independent Sector's

Megatrends & Volunteerism

Gallup Poll on Giving and Volunteering which is clearly a product of volunteerism, but we will need to explore information from far-flung corners of society which offer research that may effect how we do business in this decade and the next century.

The reading list found at the back of this book gives you a good start on a diverse group of resources that range from Alvin Toffler's *"Powershift"* to Faith Popcorn's *"Popcorn Report"*, the *Hilton Time Study Report* and even Benjamin Hoff's *"The Tao of Pooh"*!

Information bombards us every day from media and print sources and the effective volunteer administrator of the future will need to be ever-vigilant, seeking information applicable to her program.

Let me share some trends lists I've found helpful in sketching out a vision of our field's future and offer, in outline, italicized fashion, some applications I can see for volunteerism.

POWERSHIFT by Alvin Toffler:

Toffler lists eight trends in society:

1. **Demassification**:   There will be a switch to customization, value-added items, constant innovation, options.

   This trend has already popped up in volunteerism, as seen in the diversification of people and programs and a growth in entrepreneurial volunteering and multiple options of service such as flex-space, flex-time, shared-jobs, etc. It may also be seen in recognition through value-added rewards such as insurance, complimentary meals in agency cafeterias, opportunities to attend general trainings presented by the agency, skill-building, in addition to personalized recognition items.

2. **Re-define currency:** A movement toward barter, credit, electronic banking will occur.

   We will see creative bartering of services, exchange of items, expertise, etc. Time will be considered our most valuable resource and it's most prized 'investment' will be relationships.

134

Expanded Expertise

At the same time that we reach for the human touch we will need to become more familiar with electronic devises that make our life miserable at first as we struggle to learn how to use them, but will make it easier as the mouse replaces the pencil!

3. Re-define production: Our definition of production will widen to wellness/satisfaction of workers; more training before and support after, when buying products.

Building relationships will be key factors in volunteer satisfaction; this focus on relationships will extend to self in the form of wellness issues for volunteers and staff. Volunteering as a source of wellness will become a benefit offered in recruitment and will be entwined into the concept of service-learning when program leaders and educators see the correlation between early volunteering and life-long affinity to community service.

Relational considerations will also prompt volunteer program executives to become experts in climate...the feeling of a workplace....and sensitivity for the personal feelings of workers. In domino fashion this will then impact recruitment and retention, as satisfied volunteers spread the word of a healthy climate and good place to work to others.

4. Individual Data: Infinite data will become available via computers regarding individuals; this will help us understand patterns of interaction and segments of society.

Volunteer program executives will need to personally learn about data-gathering and interpretation and where to find true experts in this area. Armed with infinite details, the recruitment and support of volunteers will be much more precise; marketing will take on a whole new importance as volunteer leaders pour over information in order to identify targeted segments and potential markets.

Don't be shocked to have list company representatives knocking at your door in an attempt to purchase your list of volunteers, and , on the other side of the coin, also offering to rent you lists of people who are potential volunteers for you as predicted by their past involvement's with like organizations or causes.

135

In the age of information-at-its-extreme, we may see the day when you can punch the name of any potential volunteer into a computer and have it spit out their entire life pattern...of volunteering, membership, donations, financial worth, education and family information and almost more than you ever wanted to know about their personality, success in work circles, and activity patterns. (This will also affect how you screen people who have access to such files.)

5. **Death of bureaucratic thinking:** Information will be available to all, not a few; we will see 'touch-and-go' work patterns.

Projects will bring people together to work on a specific effort. When finished, the people will disband to go onto other efforts with new people. Because time is so valuable, volunteers will often shy away from any long-term assignments, and instead, turn to shorter commitments. The entrepreneurial spirit of 'see a need, meet it' will prevail with more and more people, causing the volunteer program executive to divide work assignments into two categories: Continuing (such as a hospital volunteer working in the gift shop for a year) and Project-Centered (such as gathering to clean up an empty neighborhood lot or bringing health-education to students in junior high school). In this second category are sub-sections of 'one-time-only' and 'span-of-time' job descriptions.

Information will empower people in such a way that some volunteers will seek you out because they have information that a need exists· which would fit into your announced agency goal; others will find ways to gather information regarding an assignment you have given them.

Bureaucratic thinking, which focuses on perpetuation, will be replaced by 'see it, fix it, move on' thinking, and little patience will be available for the idea of perpetuating existence.

6. **Smaller, specialty firms will emerge;** We will see the death of the monolith; coalitions and alliances will proliferate.

People and agencies will develop specific expertise; wise groups will assess any duplication of effort in their community

*and work to eliminate them, educating the public as to the
reasons some services are restructured.*

*Networks and coalition-building will be a necessary skill of
volunteer administrators, and true collaboration (not 'let's
pretend' ones that has one person demanding control) will be
a must.*

*A new pattern of 'partnering ' rather than 'partnerships 'will
emerge....."partnering' is much more flexible and does not
require working together on everything, just some logical and
carefully selected efforts.*

7. **Valuing of questioners:** There will be a de-valuing of
submissiveness; change will be seen as good and creativity will be
prized.

*Our traditional "Polly Do-Gooder" is truly dead and her
stereotypical inability to say 'no' is buried with her! People
who question what is happening, in order to assure themselves
that their time with a program is well-spent, will hold our feet
to the fire, causing agencies to carefully think through their
systems and efforts and justify what they are doing.*

*This will cause the volunteer administrator to hone and
develop even deeper expertise in people-handling and
interpersonal communications. It will also force agencies to
truly have their act together before launching efforts, as people
will volunteer where they can get straight answers and ethical
treatment.*

*Volunteer program executives will need to be change agents
and experts in reducing resistance to change. They will need to
see all of the people involved with their work as individual
creativity-units. "Staying within the lines" will not be attractive!*

8. **Non-central control:** Cultural groups will demand autonomy.

*There will be a growth in tribalism that will affect our
programs. Volunteer administrators and their hierarchy, will
need to understand diversity without letting diverse
characteristics divide us. They will need to become experts in*

offering tangible ways to say "I respect your uniqueness" and then move on to helping everyone focus on commonalties that accomplish the goal of the work.

Decision making will need to happen at the grass-roots levels as much as possible; volunteers will continue to demand a say in decisions that affect them, and the program leader will need a ton of expertise in diplomacy when decisions outside of their influence are handed down...in such a case it will be imperative that those affected at least have a say in how the decision is handed down to workers and carried out....this restores a sense of control.

National groups who insist on tight control of local efforts will begin to decline, as local groups & people refuse to comply. I've spoken elsewhere on the "Founder Syndrome", whereby a founder insists on complete control long after that is appropriate.......let me note here that such behavior will be challenged more than ever before as we become more vocal about such power plays.

A common sense, FORM-FOLLOWS-FUNCTION approach to actions will become a pattern. In this pattern, goals are clearly defined, then the path to that goal is mapped out through common sense and a desire for time and energy conservation......the form (system, rules, regulations, people, etc.) will then be created to empower actions leading to the goal. This spawns the "Leadershift" and "Relational Management" I've talked about elsewhere in this work.

The list of applications for each of Toffler's eight trends could go on and on, but for these pages, it seems enough to simply get you started with interpretations that apply to volunteerism.

You may find it helpful to take basic trends you find offered by others and ask your key staff, paid and non-paid, to consider them before gathering to brainstorm the "so what?" relevance to your program.

Diane Herby, who directs the Office of Volunteer Services for the

California Association of Hospitals and Health Systems, frequently schedules retreats for her large staff when they need to really examine an issue or plot a new course.

This time away allows everyone to focus on a topic and then use a free flow of conscious creativity to stimulate action plans. The retreats are a classic example of one of the new expertises needed by volunteer executives as they hone communication skills that lead to action.

THE POPCORN REPORT.....

Another source of trend information is Faith Popcorn (yes, that's really her name!) who leads her New York firm, The Brain Reserve, as it tracks dozens of information sources, including our *Grapevine, Volunteerism's Newsletter*, to monitor trends.

Popcorn is a master of trend-watching and connecting-the-dots between diverse fields. When she sees trends emerging, she shares them in her popular "Popcorn Report", primarily so that people who market products or services can respond to expressed needs and concerns.

We in the field of volunteerism and community service can learn a great deal from Popcorn's studies, as we track public thinking to create responsive programs and adjust our definitions of volunteers as they change through the years.

As we did with Toffler's writings, let's look at the trends she has documented as shaping our world, causing what Popcorn labels a "socio-quake", a time of change inspired by *"radically shifting assumptions about our past, present and future...(striking) deeper than social shakeups have in the recent American past...and transforming mainstream America."*

Cocooning: People are entrenched in the privacy and safety of their home or small, personal community to protect themselves from 'civilization'. They bring the world to them via electronic media and work to control their lives though still participate in life as much as possible.

This "bring the world to me" concept will effect how we recruit volunteers and what jobs we might offer. Volunteer program executives will need to look at creative ways to reach potential volunteers via voice mail, computer bulletin boards, cable TV, radio and possibly recruitment videos that let people get a look at how volunteers work with clients, subtle form of "advertising" our job opportunities.

Because much of cocooning is for safety reasons, recruitment will need to include assurances of safety from making mistakes by providing thorough training; options for working unassisted through technical support; conservation of energy, time and financial costs through explicit information about these resources, and concern about physical threats through explanations regarding safety measures.

Options should be available for working at home, in the office or with trusted others such as family, friends, co-workers etc..............all 'safe, protected, and offering a perception of health and survival.

Fantasy Adventures & Small Indulgences: Wanting safe amusements, such as exotic foods, amusement parks, adventures, etc.

This will shape how we recognize and reward people, finding out what they like, (such as my love for chocolate) and then offering an item or experience to feed this pleasure-center...(four Godiva truffles rather than a 2 lb. box of Fannie May, thank you!).

The desire for fantasy adventures also plays into the role of fun in volunteerism....the playful quality of life is becoming more and more sought and honored in our rough and tumble daily existence. Studies have now proven that fun and/or volunteerism is good for one's health, therefore encouraging efforts to introduce fun into volunteer work......especially when the work can be done with family or friends, thus introducing two expressed desires....relationships and meaningful work.

This trend will cause volunteer administrators to develop their creativity, and come up with a long list of fun/family/friends experiences to reward volunteer energies.....fun fairs, picnics, retreats, dinners out, roasts and toasts, trips, family portraits, potlucks, nights out, reunions, gifts for special collections, tickets to special events, etc.

Egonomics: This is a desire for customized everything, tailored exactly for the individual or team.

This factor will shape the way we design jobs, making sure it's a 'fit' between volunteer worker and the position.

It will also feed into the demand for agencies to insure that everything they do 'fits' with the mission statement and image of the organization.

In his management column recently, Tom Peters talked about the need for this image-to-practice fit in looking at the problems Sears was having in the market. He visited the plush surroundings of Sears' headquarters and sensed a major gap between Sears identity as "every-man's store" and its opulent quarters.

He then compared this image to WalMart's Spartan offices and suggested that groups examine the 'fit' of reality to image at all levels for clues to why many entities are struggling.

The same principle will be true for nonprofit, public and private groups and their volunteer departments. Do not be surprised if you, as volunteer program executive, are the only one looking at this perspective and, therefore, the first to spot any damaging discrepancy.

What others have called "the age of the individual" is part of the trend toward 'egonomics' and will demand that we offer specific and continuing recognition to individual accomplishments, thanking people directly and then their family, boss, church or temple, favorite organization, etc.

99 Lives and Cashing Out: People are juggling 99 things, becoming 'time-poor', lacking any patience with wasting time and putting quality of life as a top priority, even to the extent of willingness to taking less money to improve their life.

For volunteer programs this may mean that volunteers use work experiences in various agencies to 'try out' new experiences or build skills for a new life style, venture or living location.

I've mentioned the 'time' factor throughout this book, but it pops up (no pun intended) prominently in Popcorn's research. This will mean that volunteer program executives will need to take a long, hard look at jobs and systems to make sure they are time and energy-efficient. All activities and services must be examined for opportunities for improvement and streamlining. This is simply a variance on the Total Quality Management touted by the works of W. Edward Demming.

Also, all work will need to be broken down into segments that can be done in a short amount of time by different workers....remembering, however, to allow volunteers to handle a complete segment that makes sense to them. For those jobs which can be shared by multiple workers or teams or which can be taken off-site and worked on at home or in the office, job designs will need to be created so that they will be available when needed.

We will also need to be mindful of the ebb and flow of demands the volunteer is feeling from other parts of their lives, adjusting agency requirements accordingly when possible. This is an issue that needs to be looked at at the time of job placement. You don't want to assign a teacher who has high demands for time and energy at the beginning and end of the school year the leadership of an event held in those same time periods!

Down-Aging: People are getting older but feeling younger and may have as many years as a retiree as they had in their working years. Such folks are going to be out there by the tens of thousands soon and have a predisposition for nostalgia and remembrances of old-fashioned values.

This growing segment of our society can provide us with a rich resource of volunteers, advisors, board members, fund raisers and consultants in our work. The trick will be to have the expertise needed to adjust our efforts to their needs and characteristics.

Expanded Expertise

This will mean a sensitivity to seasons in extreme climates where wise Chicagoans retreat to points south of the Carolinas in the winter, and Tampa residents point their campers north toward Colorado, Wisconsin and upstate New York during the summer months.

It may mean a slower pace for some projects, shared work, transportation provisions, and work built around socialization opportunities.

It may mean a long list...compiled with the help of some of your older volunteers....of things the volunteer administrator can provide that will encourage retiree participation, such as:

• Background music at work stations set to easy-listing, not Rock, music.

• Reserved parking slots near well-lighted building entrances.

• Larger type on instruction sheets.

• A sensitivity to differences among tiers of older Americans. A 55 year old retiree may have more energy than a 95 year old, although the key ingredient to successful relationships with anyone is to treat them as individuals, not simply assuming or putting them all in any category.

• Daytime versus night-time assignments.

• A safe worksite, etc. etc.....

As people take better care of themselves and live longer, healthier lives, we will all have to adjust to individual strengths, expectations, levels of involvement and needs. The best way to tap this rich resource will be to do so with no generalizations or assumptions....Ask people when you have a question, and involve older volunteers in the decisions and plans that will effect them.

The wisdom and perspective that comes with age can offer volunteer programs the quickest route to success through involvement.

Megatrends & Volunteerism

Save our Society: There is a general perception by the public that America is in a mess, especially around issues of education, ecology and ethics.

> *This factor will impact our programs as volunteers look for agencies that they believe can help 'clean up the mess'. They will be aware that many groups are tackling these issues and therefore will 'shop around' for the one they think can be most effective.*

> *When they come to work for an agency that fits their concern, they will stay only as long as they feel they can trust it and its leaders and see that the resources of the organization are focused on the stated mission of the group.*

> *Because of their impatience, they will not linger silently in programs they deem inefficient or unfair. The day of the compliant, never-say-no volunteer is fading fast and we will experience more and more 'questioners', learning to value their demand for relevancy and results.*

> *The fatigue that plagues most Americans will result in a demand that we all do our best NOW and be accountable for the ecology of the earth, its resources and inhabitants.*

Vigilante Consuming and Staying Alive: This trend shows people demanding real products, benefits and accountability.

> *Our interactions with volunteers, potential recruits or donors will need to be totally open, honest and ethical, reassuring them that they can trust you personally and the program organizationally.*

> *Conflicts will need to be faced and resolved immediately; accountability must be prominently visible; any arrogance in the form of inappropriate use of power, money, influence or resources must be unacceptable; information must be shared openly; people must be involved in decisions that effect them, etc.*

> *The climate of programs will be the single most important, over-riding concern of the volunteer administrator, as it will*

144

set the stage for trust or distrust, security or fear, growth or stagnation, pleasure or displeasure and ultimately, success or failure.

All of the trends Popcorn discusses in detail in her book and updating communications, offer us clues as to what is happening in the world that may impact our work as volunteer program executives. Although her work is specifically geared to assist marketing efforts for products and services, there are thousands of learnings for our field, as she is describing the setting and influences our volunteers, paid staff, funders and clients bring to our programs. Some information she and other trend-watchers share may seem irrelevant, but careful examination may uncover small threads of connection to what we do and the people who interact with us.

Looking for connectedness can become a hobby for all of us, as we remain alert for information that can help us constantly improve our activities. It is this expertise, connecting the dots between information and our work, that may help us map the best routes to the future and success.

"Chance favors the alert mind."

THE VOLUNTEER PROGRAM EXECUTIVE AS CLIMATE EXPERT

In recent years a great deal of attention has been given over to personal wellness. Corporations and institutions have invested millions of dollars trying to help people within their structure attain wellness, and yet we still read about employees going berserk and killing co-workers and supervisors.

Of course such people are mentally ill at the time, but what questions must we ask about the organizations themselves that drove workers to such desperate measures? What responsibility must our work-place climates take for pushing people over the edge of rational response?

A critical expertise needed by the volunteer program executive is one that involves the building and maintaining of a supportive,

145

ethical, friendly and productive climate. This will include skills that will provide a positive work setting for paid staff, volunteers, clients and (would you believe?) even *ourselves!*

FEELINGS ARE FACTS, FOLKS!

Organizational Climate deals with how an organization feels to people who interact with it. The best policies and procedures will not retain workers if it doesn't feel good to them. These feelings, if expressed by a wide number of people (not just one or two who really do need to go elsewhere for a better 'fit' for themselves) should indicate to the leadership of the organization that serious assessment and possible adjustment needs to be made regarding the environment of the work place.

This means that the volunteer program executive respects expressions of people's feelings. How a person 'feels' is an honest appraisal from their perspective and should not be put down or denied. If a person feels a climate is unfriendly, rather than trying to argue that they are incorrect, it is better to find out what factors make up their perception. You may find instances that have either been misinterpreted or ones that do indeed imply unfriendliness.

In either case the matter needs to be set straight, changing what needs to be changed or clarifying the misinformation the worker has. Understanding that feelings are facts to the people experiencing them is one step of three that the volunteer administrator needs to have as they develop an expertise in climate issues. The other two steps deal with the reality that feelings shape worker satisfaction (or dis-satisfaction) and that leaders can shape feelings.

No one has more impact on the climate consistently than the leader. They set the tone, the pace, the communication style, the pleasure and the general rules of behavior for the group. I've spoken elsewhere in this book regarding my belief in what I have dubbed "Leadershift", a process that empowers logically-involved people to form a work circle around a project and sees the mantle of leadership shift to the various players in the group as their area of expertise is needed.

Expanded Expertise

Leadershift, combined with Relational Management, attention to the relationships between the workers and the assignment, mission and co-workers, will do more to frame the climate of an effort or organization than any other factors. If you have ever had to work under an authoritarian, control-obsessed or egomaniac boss, and the resulting paranoid climate, you understand what I am talking about!

Those 'rules of behavior' I spoke about before are called 'norms'....usually unwritten rules that govern behavior. They can be norms regarding organization demands, supervision, rewards, warmth and support, conflict, identity, standards, the physical setting or creativity and risk.

In each category, there are extremes on either end; creativity, for example, may be demanded or forbidden, the physical setting may be mandated to be the same for everyone (steel-cabinet gray, usually. Yuck.) or expected to be personalized to the hilt, warmth may be considered a must, with training programs to encourage it or it may be so frowned on that people who display warmth are reprimanded.

The extremes indicate a key factor that volunteer administrators can and should control: Enforcement of Norms.

How an organization deals with norms that are broken, determines in great measure, the feel of a work place. If the norm says, "everyone comes to work on time", and a new worker is late, how will the norm be enforced? Again there are two extremes....the warm fuzzy variety or the cold prickly type:

> **Warm-fuzzy:** "Sam, I noticed you coming in about 15 minutes late this morning. Was there an emergency? No?....Then I must have forgotten to tell you that we pride ourselves in always being on time... for regular work days, events, training meetings, etc. You'll see that one of the rewards we get for sticking to this pattern is that when we have gotten our work done, the boss often lets us leave early on a Friday. A couple of times last year she even gave us a couple of Friday's off as a surprise thank you for our punctuality....but we all have to have earned the reward by being on time in all that we do."

Cold-prickly: "Sam you were late this morning, 15 minutes. What's the matter with you? Don't you have enough sense to get here on time? When you're late it hurts all of us because the boss won't cut us any slack with a day off or early dismissal unless we all come in on time for everything! Don't make us sorry you're in this office, dammit!"

How we enforce our norms is a critical turning point in how workers, clients and supporters define the feel of the organization or group.

In addition to the norms and their enforcement, there are four dimensions of climate that need to be assessed as you measure your own work climate:

Energy: How much is available? Is the energy level high or low? Are there seasons of energy that ebb and flow, such as those associated with youth and seniors?

Distribution of Energy: How must energy be spent? Being creative or trying to survive? Taking risks in a trusting environment or keeping your mouth shut to avoid conflict?

Pleasure: Is simply great to come to work? Do you enjoy the surroundings, work, others? Is there a feeling that everyone is making a difference or working for naught?

Growth: Are there opportunities to 'grow' in a job, learning and stretching your horizons, or is there a perception that you must do everything by rote and in mindless fashion?

The feel of the workplace...its Organizational Climate...is a critical component for success in the 90's and beyond. It falls to the leaders of organizations to oversee and influence this climate to its most positive end, balancing the wellness of the workers and the wellness of the mission of the group.

Building and maintaining a community of workers and directing their energies toward stated goals is a delicate and difficult task that changes with the entry of every new challenge and each new participant.

148

Protectiveness, hard-headedness, defensiveness and total control must be laid aside and replaced with team-building, flexibility, problem solving and honesty in listening and responding to feelings and perceptions in the workplace.

The attitude of the volunteer program executive speaks as loudly as any operations manual ever could. If her attitude is positive, honest, caring, open and flexible, it will speak volumes about how the climate will be shaped.

The key to a productive, self-renewing climate is the expertise of the volunteer administrator as she influences the norms and their enforcement, gently and with individualized attention, toward the goal of a productive, user-friendly and positive setting for work.

People spend their time and energy where they feel rewarded, gain satisfaction, feel responsible and part of a friendly community. In other words, where they really make a difference and it just "feels good" to be there!

THE VOLUNTEER PROGRAM EXECUTIVE AND LEGAL ISSUES

The director of volunteer services will need to develop at least a working knowledge of the legal issues surrounding volunteerism and be wise enough to have a legal expert close at hand to guide them through the complexities of interpretation and application of the law.

More and more, especially when asked to sit on a Board, volunteers are carefully assessing the potential liability exposure before signing on. You as leader will need to be able to address their concerns and talk specifically about risk management, protection, etc.

The media has shared many examples of court cases where agencies, churches, etc. have been held responsible for the actions of paid or volunteer worker's inappropriate actions. As you recruit, do not be surprised if potential volunteers ask a lot of questions about your group's history and what steps it takes to prevent such problems. We are dealing with a very savvy and informed public, which is willing to ask tough questions and expect straight answers.

No program can totally protect itself from law suits. As my business partner reminds me, anyone can sue for anything. Programs can, however, constantly monitor activities that present risk and work to reduce or eliminate the risk to the greatest extent possible.

In our newsletter for volunteerism, "Grapevine", my partner and co-editor Steve McCurley (who is an attorney) continually shares risk management and legal issues such as EEOC's interpretations of the Americans With Disabilities Act, specific cases such as Hyland vs. Wonder which was a free speech issue (a government volunteer was fired for speaking out against his agency) and others which have a bearing on our field.

Volunteer program executives will have to develop an expertise in such issues, insure that professionals are readily available to assist with policy making and questions, and find sources that will constantly keep them abreast of developing issues, including:

- Screening volunteers and staff
- Background checks
- Tax issues
- Risk Management
- Americans With Disabilities Act compliance
- Free speech issues
- Donation policies
- Copyright infringement
- OSHA rules on Blood-borne Pathogens
- Firing volunteers and staff
- Libel and slander
- Insurance coverage
- National Service legislation
- Government employees as volunteers
- Hiring guidelines: what's OK to ask?
- Vulnerable client protections
- Confidentiality
- Harassment
- Agency representation
- Fair Labor Standards Act
- Allowable compensation for volunteers
- Union contracting
- Worker displacement
- Inappropriate behavior

- Requiring students to perform community service
- Workplace stress as a medical claim

....And after you've developed an expertise in all those areas, you can go on to learning how to program your VCR!!

THE VOLUNTEER PROGRAM EXECUTIVE AS SIMPLIFIER

KISS, "**K**eep **I**t **S**imple **S**tupid!", is a familiar admonition that may too harshly express an increasing demand to simplify everything from programming those VCRs (have you noticed TV programs being numbered for those of us needing easy directions?) to organizational systems.

Even the IRS has caught on and is working to simplify their forms, providing volunteers to help us out if we still can't fill out a 1099 or a ZXQ.7!

The volunteer program executive will have to bow to this demand so that efforts are economical in terms of money, time and energy and so that efforts can be explained to others in the most user-friendly, "I get it!" language possible.

Three rules of thumb that may tide you over until you can develop some real expertise in simplification of written or verbal communication:

#1: Never use quarter words when nickel words will do.

#2: A better word for communication is interpretation.

#3: Always check to see if the person you are interacting with heard what you thought you had said.

Enough said.

THE VOLUNTEER PROGRAM EXECUTIVE
AS SENSITIVITY EXPERT

Volunteer program executives will need to develop expertise in a wide range of areas having to do with sensitivity, bias, discrimination and other unacceptable actions.

Beyond simply knowing the laws as they relate to these issues, we will need to be constantly aware of subtle nuances that do not break the law but bend it noticeably!

In orienting new workers to positions in your agency, a key component must be clear guidelines on acceptable and unacceptable behavior regarding sexual or discriminatory issues.

Get very specific, offer some role play showing what is and is not acceptable. Offer solid information on diversity so that mutual respect can be built among your workers for their cultural and other differences while still focusing on commonalties.

Talk about humor and how it can unthinkingly promote negative stereotypes if used indiscriminately. One of the best trainings I've ever seen on diversity and discrimination was lead by a wonderful educator in Little Rock, Arkansas for a group of national service trainees.

She shared how sensitive she felt she was as a younger black woman with a Ph.D. to all stereotypical remarks that creep into our language until a co-worker gently pointed out a phrase she used after a particularly successful shopping trip, saying, "I really 'jewed' that salesman down!"

Her colleague, a Jewish professor, pointed out the insensitivity of her remark. In telling this story on herself to our trainees, she shared how many times, even the most sensitized among us, can allow an unthinking statement to slip into our language.

As a leader of volunteer programs, it is our job to act as alert experts monitoring language and behavior and stopping inappropriate interactions immediately. In doing so, allow for a variety of reasons for negative comments or actions. It will be critical for you to determine whether they were intentional or unintentional, planned or unplanned, and if the person offering the slight understood it to be so.

Remember President Bush offering the "V for Victory" hand signal in Australia in 1992? Obviously he did NOT understand it had a very different and vulgar meaning in that country!

Sensitivity issues can surface about sexuality, marital status, race, national origin, physical build, handicaps, religion, regional origin, education, political preference, profession, voice tones, intelligence, appearance, attire, hair length, accent, etc. etc.

It is up to leaders in positions of influence, to set an example for others to follow and to correct any insensitivity as soon as it happens. Watch closely for stereotypical thinking or assumptions and address them immediately!

THE VOLUNTEER PROGRAM EXECUTIVE AS EXPERT-TAPPER

In discussing the need to have expertise in so many areas affecting volunteer program administration, we must be careful to understand that that does NOT mean personal expertise by you, as executive, alone.

Probably the most valuable expertise you can develop is an ability to recognize when you need to call in experts on specific topics.

It would be wise for every volunteer department to have a file, by topic, of experts available for consultation when a question arises within their specialty that you cannot answer or when you simply need validation before giving a response.

These same people can be used as back-up experts when you feel you need some added muscle in persuading others of a particular point. I know of a volunteer director who was unable to convince her agency head of the need to orient and offer Hepatitis B inoculations to volunteers working in the blood lab.

Although she had the OSHA regulations mandating who was to be offered immunizations and state directives from the Health Department to the same effect, she faced a deaf ear from her boss, who insisted that "Volunteers aren't like staff...they wouldn't be in danger." My colleague argued that in the best of all worlds that might be true, but accidents do happen and the hospital should be protected from liability as well as the volunteers against any potential harm.

She was still not heard, so she asked the County Coroner to help her plead her case. He did just that, with the volunteer director present, and basically laid down some worst-case scenarios regarding what might happen if volunteers exposed to the risk actually came down with the disease. The CEO blanched, then agreed on the spot to train and inoculate at-risk volunteers, much as he had ordered to be done with paid employees having the same risk.

The CEO had heard the same plea and facts from the volunteer administrator, but, because the Coroner was considered by him to be an "expert", he was persuaded.

Consider starting a file of experts in areas such as legislation, legal issues, tax law, conflict resolution, climate, long-range planning, stress management, time management, event planning, personnel matters, benefits, diversity, discrimination, media, Americans with Disabilities Act, volunteer statistics, screening, program design and management, vulnerable clients, Medicare, finance, social services in the community, professionalism, training, adult learning, team-building, marketing, motivation, communication, change and others that might impact your work.

Yes, the list is long and getting longer every day.

The challenge is to keep up with the increasing complexities of volunteer program administration in a changing world...while absorbing as much expertise as is necessary to handle smaller questions and to know when to tap true experts.

The volunteer program executive/expert of the 90's and beyond will certainly feel the impact of the trends that demand they know more, share it clearly and use it wisely.

Chapter 9

PROFESSIONAL IMPROVEMENT & EXPANDED SPHERE OF INFLUENCE

"Whether ..a trustee, executive, staff member, an individual or corporate contributor or a volunteer at any level of service—the pursuit of quality should ultimately result in the delivery of effective, practical, and compassionate services in appropriate measures to people in need."

...Larry Kennedy,
"Quality Management in the Nonprofit World"

"Volunteer administrators must take part in the broader aspects of management that link us to the problems that are going on. We have to be the people who see on the horizon what's going to affect our work, including the social, political, and economic forces that affect the deployment of workers and the availability of services."

....Winifred Brown,
Ex. Dir., Mayor's Volunteer Center of NY.,
"The Changing Role of Volunteerism"

In the broader world in which volunteer program executives reside, there are major trends that converge into a demand that those who lead volunteer efforts do so in the most professional manner possible with quality as an obsession and influence a tool.

John Naisbitt's megatrends of "Information Society", "High Tech/High Touch", "Long Term Thinking" and "Participatory Democracy" collide with Peter Drucker's "Knowledge Age" and Faith Popcorn's "Save Our Society" plus the writings of Joel Arthur Barker, W. Edward Demming, Philip Crosby, James Kouzes, Barry

Posner, etc. etc. to reinforce the demand by the public in general and supporters in particular, that leaders be above reproach and experts in a wide range of topics.

If that sounds as though our volunteer program executive's job designs probably mention something about being "more powerful than a locomotive", you're right! I can recall many years ago I heard Michael Murray, trainer and consultant from Arlington, Texas talking about his work with major corporations and his observations regarding the challenges before managers from that arena as opposed to managers of volunteer programs..... *"Your job* (volunteer administration) *is much more difficult than theirs....you really have the toughest assignment in the world!"*

In sharing this observation with others, and seeing a puzzled look come over their face, I point out that volunteer leaders must **manage by persuasion**, where as corporate leaders can **manage by dictate**. It is interesting to note, however, that through the years, more and more corporate managers have found greater results from the softer style of persuasion, and in fact that is a basic theme running through the work of Peters and Waterman in *"In Search of Excellence"*.

However you wish to examine the challenges before volunteer program executives, they are sizable and change rapidly with the varying dynamics that impact organizations, clients, supporters, paid staff and volunteers.

To keep up with the "transforming" world which Peter Drucker writes about, volunteer administrators must constantly upgrade their professionalism, honing their skills of management, leadership, quality control and persuasion. They must find ways to take their rightful place among the other key department heads of their institutions; speak out in their wider community regarding their expertise in volunteerism so that everyone hearing them is aware that volunteer administration **is** a profession; write articles, sit on boards and in other ways be highly visible in order to influence directions others take regarding volunteers.

It also becomes the responsibility of those in the profession to draw in others. Too often I encounter volunteer administrators who seems to feel they have their job by accident, have too little higher education, are powerless and in fact think power is a four-letter word, or are rightfully paid less than other staff directors because they "only" manage volunteers.

Baloney.

Volunteer administrators frequently have more people working for them that the full institution's Personnel Department. Managing by persuasion is more difficult than managing by dictate. Degrees in our field have only recently been available, and a tiny minority of professionals are in their job because of a BS, MS or Ph.D. in volunteer management. Anyone who runs a successful volunteer services department has probably earned it ten times over by hard work, insight and diligence!

Those of us who have shed (or never had) any dis-empowering thoughts, need to be on the lookout for anyone who does, then take them back of the woodshed and have a little talk with them, because when any director of volunteer services takes such an apologetic, powerless stance, it burdens everyone else in the field.

Professionalism, therefore, it is not simply a matter of attending to your own stance, but that of a broader perspective of upgrading and empowering the entire landscape of our profession.

Let me stop here for a moment, to add one word of caution (and to probably allow Ivan Scheier, Ph.D., guru in our field and champion of spontaneous, grass-roots volunteering, to breath again!).

Although "professionalism" is demanded from those who direct volunteer efforts, not everyone seeks, has access to, or feels the need for the more formalized symbols of our profession.

I once encountered a woman in a West Virginia county where unemployment was 36%, very few inhabitants were above the poverty level and an educated person was defined as anyone with some high school training. She had organized a service for residents which was located in donated space in a church, had a 24 hour "Help" line, provided a hot lunch for children in need seven days a week, offered a food pantry, conducted continual (and highly persuasive!) campaigns for goods in kind, services and donations, managed a barter-bank so that people could trade skills and items equitably, ran a literacy program and job bank, and offered peer counseling to families. It was a wonderful program.

I don't know about you, but that sounds a lot like a combination of the Red Cross, a Volunteer Center, Crisis program, FISH and several other established efforts we all are familiar with around the country!

When I asked her about her job as Volunteer Administrator, she balked at the title. I think it sounded too foreign and "uppity" to her, and she said, "No, I'm no big shot...I just want to help my folks".

Needless to say, I did not attempt to persuade her to seek professional credentialing, join AVA, get further schooling (she had a 7th grade education), read Toffler, Scheier, Demming or Peters or any of the other symbols we recognize as marks of a professional. I simply praised her for what she was doing, took a step backwards and in my heart knew I was in the presence of greatness.... and a true "pro"!

As much as I am a champion of operating at the highest level of professionalism, I realize that it cannot and is not practical for every person running a volunteer program. There is much we can learn from the spontaneous leaders in America who never have thought that what they do could be considered a profession, and when they hear that for the first time, may even be slightly amused at the thought, but too busy being successful to ponder it too long.

I was pleased to recently come upon a quote from Katherine Noyes, President of the professional organization in the field, the Association for Volunteer Administration, as she spoke to the same point:

> *"There's a vast quantity of informal, independent, spontaneous volunteering that is occurring all over the place. Yet often we act as if we're the only game in town. Some of the emphasis on professionalism has produced a*

> *rigidity in some of our organizations. If we are to accomplish all that we strive for, we must be open to working with this other world of volunteer activity instead of controlling it or recruiting it or forcing it to become part of our formal structure. We must do a better job of creating true networks, not hierarchies or predetermined slots."*

.... *"The Changing Role of Volunteerism*

Now that I'm out of trouble with Ivan Scheier, and probably in trouble with those who tout the cry of "professional credentials for ALL!", let's go back to looking at how we go about upgrading our personal and collective professionalism..........

INFLUENCING OTHERS....THE ART OF CLOUT!

No, clout is **not** a bad word. It means having influence; being able to persuade; asserting a stance, and working to leverage the respect others have for you to better the position of the volunteer department in working toward the mission of the organization.

Thinly disguised, it is the art of marketing, deciding what and who you need, then strategizing to attain your need. The four questions mentioned previously; 1: What do you HAVE?, 2: What do you NEED?, 3: WHO HAS what you need?, and 4: HOW can you get what you need?

To begin to gain clout, I believe volunteer program executives (A phrase I use to attempt to raise the level of appreciation of all that you must do and be. You are executives, not simply managers, administrators or directors) must individually and collectively help erase any misconception that they are simply clerical workers and no more professional than being the inexperienced president of a small ladies-aide club!

☞ If you are excluded from department head meetings, find a way to sit in to offer support or information. Then use the opportunity to show how valuable your presence is by offering connectedness with each department as they report on activities and needs. Offer assistance or questions that will

159

prompt an "ah-Ha!" in other executive's thinking when they are discussing new projects and you see an opportunity to interject volunteer energies to make it successful.

☞ If, during a money crunch, you see a disproportionate cut from your budget, gather facts on how the volunteers make the institution more cost effective, the value of volunteer time nationally, the impact volunteers have on public opinion and therefore potential supporters, and the statistics showing the giving patterns of volunteers versus non-volunteers. Then present your case logically, factually and with alternate suggestions of where cuts might be made that will not "gut" your department.

> At Rex Hospital in Raleigh, NC, the volunteers themselves were asked for suggestions on ways in which the hospital might save money. They promptly offered several that ended up saving Rex $50,000 per year! Needless to say, the Director of Finance is now a strong supporter of the volunteers in the hospital.

☞ If you find you are being paid more like a clerical worker than a department head, gather more facts to demonstrate the worth of the volunteers to the organization, the professional skills you have and need to direct all the energies of the human resources under your leadership, and your true role as internal consultant to others throughout the organization.

Such demonstrations of an attitude that says you are a "second-class citizenry" must be addressed, first by examining your own attitudes regarding your position and professionalism. If you are projecting a message of, _"ah shucks, I'm just glad to be working with these great volunteers"_, it is time to take a hard look in the mirror and offer yourself a little lecture on how good and important what you do and who you are is to the whole organization!

BUILDING PERSONAL CREDIBILITY

In their wonderful little book, _Building Credibility With The_

Professional Improvement & Expanded Sphere of Influence

Powers That Be, authors Gail Moore and Marilyn Mackenzie suggest that:

> "_Personal credibility starts with YOU. Before others will value you and your services, you must first believe in and value them yourself. What is your personal vision? What beliefs and values express your personal philosophy? Challenge yourself to think about the personal vision that drives you._"

They then go on to help volunteer program executives examine their self-perceptions by asking them to fill in the blanks of the following:

---

1. This is what I believe about myself as a person...............

2. This is what I believe about volunteerism......................

3. This is what I believe about volunteers...........................

4. This is what I believe about managing volunteers..................

5. This is what I believe about working in a social service agency (school, arts, rehab, etc.)..........

6. This is what I believe about clients in this organization..........

After filling in the blanks on these 6 questions, the authors instruct readers to think through the same statement for each of the 6: **"Because I believe as I do, therefore this is how I behave....."**

That little exercise may help you to uncover your feelings and subsequently, what you project to others. Keep in mind the old admonition: _"What you do speaks so loudly, I cannot hear what you say."_

On the road of professionalism, you must first root out your own attitudes, your relationship to yourself and others around you, before you can assess how best to build your credibility with others.

We then need to look at how others see us, assessing how we present ourselves physically in dress, demeanor and appearance. As much as we would like for others to judge us only on our internal self, it simply does not happen that way. The volunteer program executive dressed appropriately in suit or classic outfit will command more credibility than one in sloppy jeans or (God forbid!) spandex shorts.

Only you can decide what is appropriate for your organization. The climate can vary from group to group, but whatever it is, dress as the executive you are! (and no spandex allowed, thank you.)

As spoken of at length in the Expanded Expertise chapter of this book, knowledge is critical to the professional appearance of volunteer program executives! Being a font of information that many people in your organization can tap into, will do more to enhance your credibility than any other single thing. When you are perceived as a valuable and practical resource of knowledge, what you say in any setting will more readily be heard.

Other attributes of your professional standing that Moore and Mackenzie speak to include:

- Showing respect for others.
- Demonstrating honest and ethical behavior.
- Recognizing that you have much to offer (without being a "know-it-all").
- Setting a good example in standards of quality of work.
- Showing a warm and caring attitude with others.
- Being sensitive to the needs of others.
- Collaborating with others.
- Being loyal to people so they know they can trust you.
- Celebrating the success of others.

In a paper by the United Hospital Fund of New York, *The Changing Role of Volunteerism,* speakers at a conference of the same name listed additional suggestions for building professionalism and credibility:

1. Develop expertise in other fields beyond volunteerism.
2. Put on different hats to serve the broader organization when possible.

162

3. Communicate regularly with the board of trustees and staff in other departments.
4. Orient new employees about the volunteer program.
5. Work to build linkages with other community agencies and groups.
6. Speak at conferences and meetings.
7. Document and publish new and innovative work to help others replicate it.

To these I would add: keeping up to date on information effecting your work and the mission of the organization; attending to the nurturing of the climate of your worksite; building and tapping networks that can support your work; reading, learning and translating information constantly; being open to criticism and testing it for its validity; taking the "long-view"; continually searching for information from the field that you can pass on to the CEO and board; getting your organization's librarian to obtain major periodicals and works from our field.

The list could go on, but I'd rather stop here to let you add your own ideas.

CREDENTIALING

One last note on personal credibility and professionalism:

Explore the opportunities that exist to enhance your professional standing through credentialing programs offered by many organizations.

The Association for Volunteer Administration, the professional association for all varieties of paid and non-paid volunteer program executives around the world, offers a CVA (Certified Volunteer Administrator).

"The certification process is open to all volunteer administrators who have at least two years' experience. Among the requirements for the certificate are a 200-word statement of philosophy and a longer narrative, which are reviewed by a panel that then suggests additional reading or coursework."(Winifred Brown, United Hospital Fund of New York, *The Changing Role of Volunteerism.*)

Other, niche-specific (keep in mind the "niche focus" trend reported by Faith Popcorn) groups offer credentialing and learning for volunteer executives in hospitals and health care, criminal justice, schools, fundraising, etc. etc. Scout out the opportunities to acquire professional credentialing; investigate the process and decide on suitability to your situation.

CREDIBILITY OF THE VOLUNTEER DEPARTMENT

After looking at personal credibility, it is critical to examine the credibility of the volunteer department. To have real clout, the department must:

☞ Contribute to the achievement of the agency or organizational mission.

☞ Effectively manage the volunteer resource.

☞ Offer real work that helps staff succeed.

☞ Mentor systems that empower success and goal attainment.

☞ Celebrate success and growth.

☞ Become valuable to all aspects of the organization through internal consultancy roles.

THE CURRENCY OF IDEAS

In boosting professionalism and clout, and constantly improving quality, we find a new ally in an often-overlooked resource.

As our perspectives expand surrounding the definition of resources, we find several new items listed as valuable in addition to money and goods:

- Time
- Energy
- Information

To this list I would add what I see as a new currency of the 90's and beyond:

. . .IDEAS!

My conclusion comes from the endless list of writers...Covey, Drucker, Naisbitt, Popcorn, et al...who point to the information age in which we live.

They also parallel a new, very revolutionary theory in economics, proposed by Paul Romer, Ph.D., a professor of economics at the University of California at Berkeley and reported in the Chicago Tribune, May 17, 1993.

His premise is that the economic growth of nations is in direct correlation to the IDEAS it comes up with and that future growth and development can be predicted by monitoring countries' ideas which he believes are the major engines of growth.

Just as Romer attributes knowledge and the ideas it generates as the factor for growth in nations, I believe the same factor will empower programs' growth.

Because organizations need all the help they can get to survive and thrive into the next century, this puts the volunteer service executive in a potentially powerful position. By using information to create ideas that integrate volunteers at all levels of work, the volunteer services department can fuel the growth and strengthen the entire organization.

Think about it.

☞ If volunteer executives can come up with new ideas to attract, integrate and empower volunteers to augment staff efforts, thereby increasing energy, synergy and effectiveness, the organization will be that much more effective in accomplishing it's mission.

☞ If the volunteer services department can model the best characteristics of leadership, empowerment, community, accountability, mission-focus, wellness and systems-design, **IT** becomes the leader facet of the entire agency and establishes credibility at the highest executive levels.

The effective DVS of 2000 a.d. will carefully gather, nurture, invest, monitor and expend the currency of ideas so that the return on the investment strategies compounds to the most fruitful yields of increased effectiveness, credibility and expanded influence.

As master communicator and team builder, the DVS of the future will be ever-vigilant for new information and ideas, rewarding and coaching those who share them to come up with even more.

CRITICAL SUCCESS FACTORS

For others to appreciate what the volunteer program executive director does and is, success must surround their work and their own person.

Years ago I ran across an article by Charles Garfield, Ph.D. listing the six characteristics of successful people. They:

1. Do not blame...they problem solve.
2. Avoid comfort zones...they grow.
3. Work for the "art" of it.
4. March to an internal drumbeat.
5. Take risks..they imagine the worst and map how to cope.
6. Rehearse mentally...they picture success.

Garfield's research of thousands of successful men and women from all fields of endeavors also showed that they are NOT workaholics.

Stephen Covey, in his best seller, *The 7 Habits of Highly Effective People*, listed the following as critical to effective, or successful people:

1. Being proactive.
2. Beginning with the end in mind.
3. Putting first things first
4. Thinking "win-win".
5. Seeking first to understand, then to be understood.
6. Synergizism..creative melding of multiple ideas.
7. Continual improvement (what Covey called "sharpening the saw").

In a later book, *Principle-Centered Leadership,* he took these 7 habits and fleshed them out as human endowments that leaders such as those in volunteerism might adopt as they lead organizations and people into the 21st century:

1. Proactiveness demands that the leader have self-knowledge or self-awareness
2. To begin with the end in mind takes imagination and conscience.
3. Putting first things first requires willpower and a focused discipline.
4. Thinking 'win-win' demands an abundance-mentality rooted in principle-centered security that says there is enough power, profit and recognition to go around and you don't have to hoard it all; that capacity outweighs incapacity; that mutual benefit is good and self-worth is intrinsic.
5. Seeking first to understand takes courage balanced with consideration and empathy.
6. Synergism requires creativity for solutions through collaborative thinking; coming up with better solutions together than what could have been devised individually.
7. "Sharpening the saw" demands continuous improvement and self-renewal.

I list all these ways to measure success here because it touches on a basic principle I believe all signs point to as critical to being able to thrive in the days and years ahead:

Leaders must identify critical success factors in all they DO and ARE in order to map a path toward ultimate effectiveness and professionalism.

Pressures of accountability, cries for ethical actions, attention to values and a need for the ecology of time and energy, all demand that efforts be as effective, as focused, as possible on the mission of the organization or effort.

To do this, leaders will have to identify those conditions or factors which must be present to help bring about success. Beyond simply the goal or vision, there are specific factors against which all actions are measured, that help define to all involved or observing, what must happen for the effort to be successful. They provide a road map for people to follow.

In working to empower success in one of the pilot programs authorized by the Commission on National and Community Service through the National and Community Service Act of 1990, Steve McCurley and I mapped out critical success factors for the Delta Service Corps, a 1000-member corps of stipended community service volunteers serving counties and parishes along the Mississippi River in Arkansas, Mississippi and Louisiana.

Because each program has its own unique circumstances, and must therefore decide on what it considers to be it's own success factors, there is no laundry list generic to every effort. Let me share, therefore, the list for the Delta Service Corps simply as an example of factors that had to be in place for it to be successful:

DELTA SERVICE CORPS..Critical Success Factors:

1. Recruitment of participants must be disciplined and uniform throughout.
2. Standards, policies & procedures must be set realistically for participant involvement.
3. Systems must enable, not stymie, those involved.
4. Site leaders must be properly trained to receive and assimilate participants positively.
5. Training and direction must be job-specific, clear, experiential, practical and come from audience-acceptable leaders.
6. Expectations must be clearly articulated in non-punitive manner and be realistic.
7. Information must be easy to access and complete.
8. Reward systems must reinforce positive behavior.
9. Workers must appreciate that the DSC enables them to serve through their site placement, and loyalty must be aligned to both entities.
10. Workers must see their primary goal as community service with post-service rewards a secondary factor.
11. Leadership must be undivided in its attention to the needs of the DSC.
12. Everyone musts be clear on what their role is and how it effects the DSC success.

13. Everyone must understand, be able to articulate and work toward the mission of the DSC.

Of all the megatrends that shape our work in volunteerism, none may be as important as accountability and no tool more valuable than a well-crafted definition of critical success factors.

SERVANT LEADERSHIP

When working to build credibility with those above, below or in parallel to you on someones' old-fashioned management chart, I can think of no better place to begin than with the work of Robert Greenleaf, who until his death in 1990, wrote and spoke about his concept of "Servant-Leadership". His phrase, less of an oxymoron than a sort of Zen koan, is really just a juxtaposition of apparent opposites intended to startle you and force you to have to think long and hard about the two words.

The concept is that the leader exists to serve those that he or she leads.

There are five principles to Greenleaf's work, which, when taken to heart, can offer a rather clear road map for increased credibility:

1. The leader takes people and their work very seriously, respecting and honoring them and working to empower their good works as authentic individuals.

2. The leader listens and responds to the expressions of the followers, asking questions and working to not always impose answers; the art of consensus-building is highly prized and used often by the leader. This attitude leads to continual quality improvement, marrying it with Demming's work on Total Quality Management.

3. The leader heals, working to make whole those wounds that occur; he or she is not afraid to openly share mistakes and pain, and does not run from "grief-work" in any setting.

4. The leader is self-effacing, never reading or believing press-clippings; glorifying leadership is NOT a goal!

169

5. The leader takes on the role and attitude of steward, pondering what has been entrusted to them; the leader brings vision but carefully listens to the vision of others, engaging those people directly affected by the choices to be made and coming up with a shared vision which is better than any one opinion.

Servant-leadership listens to what everyone has to say, draws out the best ideas, then adds a clear vision and soft management posture. All of this together defines the servant-leader who is a strong, selfless steward, determined to help others be the best they can be.

And if that doesn't sound a lot like the typical, highly effective volunteer services executives of this world, I don't know what does!

HELPING YOUR ORGANIZATION AVOID PITFALLS

If you truly want to go to the head of the class of building credibility, help your organization sidestep the mistakes so many nonprofit groups make. In a wonderful little pamphlet by Brian O'Connell entitled *"For Voluntary Organizations In Trouble or Don't Want To Be"*, Brian offers his observations from many years of helping groups who find themselves in trouble.

His list of danger signals include:

A failure to focus on mission and priorities, with people being side-tracked. This goes back to my exercise, which I find Brian uses also, of asking key leaders in an organization to write down their mission, then watching to see different answers arise. It clearly identifies a group in trouble...rather like beginning a trip wondering what all the confusion is when everyone has a different destination.

A failure to invest in building the board is a particular horror story for Brian who has done so much to help organizations strengthen and guide the trustee-arm of groups. Too little time is given to searching for the right people, cultivating their interest and preparing for their work if and when they agree to join the board. A sub-category of this issue is confusion between the role of the board and that of the staff, which must be clear and workable, and explained carefully to any new staff or board members when they come aboard.

Role confusion about the chief volunteer officer, and **the trustee roles of board members versus other efforts as individual volunteers,** can also point to problems in an organization. Watch for problems that are rooted in murky definitions of who does what and when. They can be deadly when people continue to trip over varying definitions of assignments and you hear phrases such as, *"it must have slipped through the cracks"* or *"but I thought YOU were going to do that!"* .

Financial concerns can signal trouble for any size group. Deficits and lack of funds are almost a sure road sign for drained energies, stress, confusion and uncertainty. Whatever it takes to ethically get back on sound financial footing must be a priority. Often it takes someone outside of the treasurer's office or the development department to see that a lot of problems have their roots in over-taxed financial demands. In-fighting, bickering, suspicions, etc. can frequently be tracked back to too little operating funds and high competition between departments for money.

Problems can come from **right people being in wrong jobs**. An executive director or leader who simply is not a match with your organization; board members who are single-issue driven and refuse to become involved in the total organization; board or staff leaders who will not deal directly with conflict and permit a Pollyanna mentality that ignores small problems until they are a disaster; failure of executives to honestly evaluate progress and measure efforts against the mission for fear of offending anyone..(the "don't make waves" school of management).

Lack of open information is another symptom of an organization in trouble so that full disclosure is restricted. Another variation on this same theme is failure to live up to legal and moral responsibilities in our age of demand for ethical operations.

The volunteer program executive cannot "fix" any of these problems that might arise...that is not part of her job description, but she can watch for signs of trouble and alert top leadership of possible areas for concern. If she can also suggest remedies for the problems and become a valuable member of any task-groups assigned remediation, her credibility will go up dramatically, and her professionalism respected by those in authority.

I suppose this might be characterized as the Paul Revere attribute, keeping in mind that it is good old Paul that was immortalized in poetry, not the British or colonists who fought the subsequent battle!

TEN TIPS FOR CREDIBILITY

I'll leave the topic of building professional credibility with some tips I have picked up from working with hundreds of highly professional, credible, authentic, strong volunteer program executives. No matter who or where they are, whether they run programs in zoos, museums, hospitals, Army bases, churches, or social service agencies, they seem to repeat a pattern of attitude and action that makes everyone around them sit up and take notice, honoring them as a true servant-leader, and following them wherever they go:

These incredible people, easily found in our field....

☞ Have vision..for themselves, their department and their organization.

☞ Are a passionate advocate for volunteerism.

☞ Build programs to better serve client needs.

☞ Set good examples. In **every** way.

☞ Know their stuff and work to keep on learning and growing.

☞ Become involved in planning, internally and externally.

☞ Build collaborative relationships on trust and reliability.

☞ Seek out and connect with supportive allies.

☞ Understand and leverage political & power networks.

172

☞ Value the contributions others and THEY THEMSELVES make!

☞ They are real and they care.

> *"Grant me that I am human; that I hurt and I can cry."*...Gwendolyn Brooks

TIPS TO DEMONSTRATE PROFESSIONAL AUTHENTICITY

A simple list of additional ways to impact others:

1. Articulate how volunteers are a critical/integral part of the organization.
2. Clip relevant articles and sent to CEO, the Board, etc.
3. Suggest you can help with Board orientation.
4. Look for opportunities to talk about volunteers.
5. Stress accountability.
6. Make Volunteer Week a real, agency-wide celebration.
7. Help staff express appreciation for volunteers and vice-versa.
8. Inspire others: articulate your vision as supportive to agency vision.
9. Leverage influence.
10. Build commitments.
11. Identify "agents" or "authenticators" who will speak on your behalf.
12. Keep up to date with trends that impact volunteers & service.
13. Build wider credibility in your community for the department & agency.
14. Follow the 11th Commandment: **Thou Shall Get Thy ACT Together!**

THE GRANDMOTHER FACTOR

In the field of volunteerism the idea of female leadership is the norm as women have the vast majority of positions as directors of volunteer services.

Megatrends & Volunteerism

The softer style of management, often characterized as "feminine", is fast becoming the appropriate style for the 90's and beyond and there are few other professions that already display this style more naturally than ours.

Men across the country are taking seminars to help them be more sensitive, persuasive and relational, and the men and women who already display this style are being propelled to leadership positions.

In a Chicago Tribune article of May 16, 1993, Swedish sociologist Per Gahrton suggested that female values could even rescue the world!

Gahrton stated that, *"Ten thousand years of male domination have brought the human race to the brink of ruin and it may not survive unless it quickly adopts more feminine values."*

He went on to say there are: *"seven deadly sins of male-dominated society: capitalism, colonialism, communism, militarism, urbanism and the perverted used of biology and technology. I reason that the opposite pole to this in human terms is the Grandmother."*

It probably won't surprise you that his book, *"Let Grandmothers Rule the 2,000's-A Book About Our Future"* is available for further reading on this subject.

In their book, *"Megatrends For Women"*, authors Patricia Auberdene and John Naisbitt, devote all of their energies to examples of the move toward feminization of systems, organizations, movements and politics:

"Male-dominated institutions from the US Senate to the Hierarchy of the Roman Catholic Church will be dragged kicking and screaming into the 21st century," they tell us.

Backing this statement up by inexhaustible statistics, Aburdene and Naisbitt refer to the "critical mass" theory in physics which basically says that when enough energy collects in one spot and is then sparked, it takes on a momentum of its own and cannot be contained.

That may have been the reason that the Catholic Cardinal from Chicago, Joseph Bernadin, held a press conference in mid-June of

1993 to announce that from that point on into the next century, the Church under his control would adopt a softer, more "listening and responsive" attitude with parishioners in an effort to stop them from leaving their parishes in droves and to *"possibly convince some of those already gone that they can come back into the community of the faithful with full confidence in the Church"*.

He pointedly spoke of his desire to have female altar-servants and the role of women heightened in worship, and addressed directly his commitment to removing any and all clergy or lay leaders who have any history or suggestion of sexual impropriety. He established a hot-line direct to his office for any parishioners to report misconduct and assured his followers that they would be fairly heard and not ignored as they had been in the past. (At the time he spoke, 22 priests from the Chicago area were under investigation or indictment for sexual misconduct with children.)

The Cardinal's words sound like a Grandmother's assurances to me and reflect back to the need society expresses for safety and ethical treatment.

Around the world, the feminization of life and work has reached that critical mass point and thereby, has caught up with the field of volunteerism which has been at that state all along!

The reason this is critical to us now is that we are entering an age when the traditionally female volunteer service executive will work with and for men and women who also display the characteristics of the softer, feminine style of leadership that are:

- Soft rather than harsh; persuasive rather than dictatorial; team-building rather than militaristic; relational rather than hierarchical; empowering rather than authoritarian.

- Integrated, not closed; help-seeking rather than Lone-Rangerish; inclusive, not exclusive.

- Practical versus theoretical; consensus building vs. ivory-tower decision-making; hands-on vs. hands-off; wholistic vs. fractional, and accountable vs. arrogant.

Megatrends & Volunteerism

As the feminine management style gains acceptance and even prominence, the profession of volunteer administration will grow.

Volunteer program leaders will have more respect; be seen as examples of effective management; and as respected executives.

As in all opportunities for growth, there are some dangers to be avoided:

1. ***No Prima-Donnas allowed!*** New respect would evaporate quickly if a DVS began to demand special privileges or exemption from rules everyone else has to follow.

2. ***Arrogance is OUT!*** Accountability will need to remain one of the foundation stones for any manager or executive. Any graduates of the Atilla the Hun School of Management need not apply.

3. ***Mad-dog Management is a No-No!*** If you have ever run into anyone who cannot distinguish the difference between being assertive or being aggressive, you'll understand my Mad-dog analogy. There are effective ways, within the feminine style of management, to present a case assertively and forcefully without becoming rabid.

4. ***No Whining Allowed:*** There are some who believe feminine style management means baby-doll voices, asking by apology, submissiveness and conflict-avoidance. They are wrong. Period. Strong women refuse to be victims and also do not try to manipulate through a subservient posture.

The underlying issue in how America will put knowledge to good use through contemporary management executives, is **COMPETENCE**, getting things done effectively. Competence by making the mission happen; designing systems that empower people to achieve success; insuring quality; improving constantly; learning and growing; building community.

In the 1990's every trend-writer from Naisbitt to Popcorn, Peters to Drucker, Aburdene to Baker and Toffler to Covey, speak of the need for a softer style of management. A more feminine, intuitive, wholistic, inclusive, communitarian, empowering, relational approach to getting things done.

Quite possibly this shift, at this time of critical mass, means the people, both male and female, in the field of volunteer management, are in a profession whose time has finally come!

> *"To be persuasive we must be believable; to be believable we must be credible; to be credible, we must be truthful"*
>
> ..Edward R. Murrow

Megatrends & Volunteerism

Chapter 10

CHANGING ROLES OF VOLUNTEER PROGRAM EXECUTIVES

"Trust is almost always needed when leaders are accomplishing extraordinary things in organization."
. ...James Kouzes & Barry Posner,
"The *Leadership Challenge*"

"Thinking about power makes us apprehensive. Power corrupts, power is violence. We forget the d i f f e r e n c e between power used to manipulate others and power used to empower others. Power is a neutral force; we control the quality of its use."
.....Jennifer James,
"Success is the Quality of Your Journey"

All of the trends that surround us as a nation have an impact on the work of directing volunteer efforts. As the rapid pace of change escalates in the wider world, we find ourselves having to adapt to the impact of those changes on our daily work and the roles we play in leading volunteer energies.

Unlike all the other chapters in this book, here, in this last offering, I want to simply share some specific roles I see volunteer program executives taking on, as indicated by the dozens of books and articles I read for background for this work. In certain instances I will share a major influence in my thinking, either in the way of a specific trend or trend-watcher who spoke to the topic.

For the most part, however, I will simply share what I have observed, read or experienced that is the basis for my conclusions, so that I can get to the meat of what the role may be and you can avoid having your eyeballs swirl at all the footnotes! No role spoken of here is suggested by a single source....instead, it appears here because it has so MANY sources!

WE'LL STOP MANAGING VOLUNTEERS!

Without a doubt, the role of the director of volunteers, which for decades meant hands-on, side-by-side interactions with volunteers, is changing. We now see these same volunteer professionals redirecting their focus toward interactions with staff and hierarchy to facilitate smooth integration of volunteers into management and service-delivery systems.

> When Mary Wiser took over as Director of Volunteers at the Courage Center near Minneapolis in 1977, she found a small number of volunteers at the rehabilitation facility restricted to working in very few, non-essential jobs.
>
> Her naturally friendly and nurturing ways lead her to a quick bonding with the volunteers while at the same time, she was observing the relationships of the staff to those volunteers, her department as a management entity, and one another.
>
> After careful observation and interpretation....a period characterized by the mother-of-the-groom rule of "wear beige and keep your mouth shut"....it became clear that there was great room and need for expansion of volunteer services throughout the Center IF those in charge of various departments could be convinced of the competency and accountability of volunteers.
>
> With a solid faith in the miracles that correctly placed and trained volunteers can bring about, Mary set out to remove any barriers to volunteer utilization as diligently as the Courage Center worked to break down barriers for those clients struggling with debilitating physical conditions.

First she became personally familiar with each department director, their needs, responsibilities, histories with the Center, strengths and management style. If they had reservations regarding volunteers, she listened patiently and without defensiveness, to their concerns.

Next she identified the respected leaders among the various groups at the Center. Without a need to label it as such, she had adopted a philosophy of marketing the volunteer program to identifiable groups..."publics"...within the Center. Quick to spot those who could influence others, she established genuine, caring relationships with each. (administrative staff, leadership, medical staff, patients, client families, etc.), listening to their concerns and ideas as to how volunteers might assist their needs and goals. In short, she took the "Servant-Leader" stance, putting in practice a philosophy of leadership that says those who wish to lead must be willing to first serve.

With a clear and intense focus on her goal of increasing volunteer effectiveness throughout the Center, she began to design strategies and practical plans of action. Each plan was based on how to best respond to expressed needs of key staff so that volunteer energies were focused on helping staff be successful. Often she would identify a highly competent volunteer and then talk to a department supervisor about his or her credentials, waiting for the supervisor to suggest brining them into their work.

At the same time she began to build partnerships with other department heads, watching again for opportunities to offer volunteer support to help facilitate their goals. She also began building a staff that managed different specialties among volunteers, expanded the communications network to increase visibility of volunteer contributions, established an extremely effective and powerful advisory committee, emphasized volunteer recognition and training, and established a climate that encouraged creativity and team approaches to problem solving.

Problems were reframed as challenges, resistance as opportunities for re-education, and closed doors as exciting adventures-in-waiting.

The results of Mary's focus on creating and empowering systems within a caring and creative climate that would effectively integrate volunteers into all aspects of the Center's operation were outstanding. In 1990, the year Mary left to establish her own management consulting firm, she traveled to Washington, DC with the chair of the Volunteer Advisory Board to accept the President's Award for Outstanding Voluntary Action for the program at the Center.

By that time, the program at the Courage Center boasted 2000+ volunteers working in every department of the vast complex. Volunteer jobs ranged from office work to running a gift store of client's handicrafts to inventive "tinkerers" and engineers devising toys and equipment adapted to client's capabilities......all essential jobs!

The Courage Center, by this time, regarded the volunteer department as a driving force integrated naturally into every aspect of its operation. The volunteer department was seen as equal in status and importance to every other department, and volunteer workers and leaders were respected and accepted as part of the team willing and able to serve client's needs.

The success of the Courage Center's volunteer department is a testimony to a growing understanding by volunteer program executives that the focus needs to be on strategies and systemic relationships that enhance and empower volunteers, paid staff, clients and supporters to work together toward the goal of the organization.

On occasion, it is necessary for volunteer administrators to roll up their sleeves and help volunteers actually carry out work assignments, but for the most part, their time is better spent working to influence those in authority of the credibility of the department, volunteer contributions and the overall success of the organization. In short, to manage the climate and systems that surround and support volunteer efforts rather than managing every little action of the volunteers themselves.

For those who manage small programs, this may seem like a fantasy, but I would suggest that attention to "growing" the volunteer department's status and acceptance in even the tiniest of organizations will probably set the stage for a decided increase of satisfied volunteers who tell friends of their enjoyable work and therefore recruit even larger numbers. All this translates into clout to bring on paid or non-paid staff workers assigned to tend to the daily responsibilities of volunteers themselves. .. a multiplying factor critical to our field if we are to keep up with the megatrends that surround us.

LEADERSHIFT AND RELATIONAL MANAGEMENT

All of the preceding hints at what I believe will be a shift in how directors of volunteer programs lead and manage by the turn of the century and beyond. The external trends that shape our work, the changes we see in the people, institutions and needs surrounding us, will demand a new approach to working with and through others to accomplish dreams.

I believe that what I have called **"Leadershift"** will be adopted more and more; a flexible, fair, fast-paced and future-oriented way of dealing with assignments, that shifts people in and out of work circles according to the strengths and gifts each can bring to the task at hand.

> *Leadershift: The philosophy of assembling people around a work assignment according to the need for their expertise, and then empowering each person to take the leader role when the focus is on their specific perspective.*

> *Work groups are then disbanded when their shared goal is accomplished, with individuals re-assigned to other efforts where their expertise is again needed.*

It also draws on any variety of management and leadership philosophies that seem appropriate for the assignment, thus allowing the ultimate leader to avoid being locked into any one theory or management-trick-of-the-day trap.

Leadershift establishes a climate of acceptance and respect for the contributions of others and understands that it takes a variety of skills and perspectives to produce the highest quality work.

183

For example, when putting together a Well-Baby clinic in a small rural community, the ultimate leader of the effort (There is always an "ultimate leader", often a visionary, who takes overall responsibility for making a dream a reality) using "Leadershift" would gather a small group of people who have a stake in the success of the clinic....the local doctor, a mid-wife, the Head Start director, a high school guidance counselor, an expectant mother, the parents of small children, a town council member, service group leaders, ministers, etc.

All would have expressed an interest in such a clinic from different perspectives and accepted an invitation to attend an exploratory meeting to discuss bringing the dream of better health for small children to reality. (Note the vision is of better health for children NOT the clinic itself.)

The ultimate goal would be broken down into manageable parts, and "work circles" would be drawn around such essential components as fund raising, site, staff, permits, etc. Those involved would be able to see an outline of all the parts and circles so that they have an over-all picture of what needs to be accomplished to reach the goal and how all the parts fit together.

Each circle of work would be based around logical divisions of labor. Members of the circle would be those who have special expertise, a relationship to, and stake in, the ultimate goal. By shifting the mantle of leadership from circle member to circle member when their aspect becomes critical, each would take their shift as leader....thus: **LEADERSHIFT.**

> ***The ultimate leader*** *of the entire effort would then step back, out of the way, to turn her attention toward nourishing the climate and providing systems that facilitate success, inspire creative solutions, increase program quality and guarantee respect from those whose support, cooperation and permission is needed.*

In case that sounds a bit muddy, let me offer some other examples:

When the walkathons were first being developed by Project Concern in the late 1960s and early 1970s in America, I was involved in a pioneering effort in San Diego, the headquarters of this

184

international health care and training organization for which I worked.

Thousands of walkers showed up on walk day and hiked the 20 mile route which we believed to be the most beautiful one anyone had _ever_ seen, culminating above the wonderful sand beach of that great city.

At an evaluation meeting held later to examine the success of the walk, we knew we had some things to remedy regarding check-points, crowd control, certificates and sponsor collection so we opted to begin the meeting by asking for feedback on the route, a surefire way (we believed) to start the meeting off on a positive, "lets-gloat-at-our-brilliant-mapping" note.

So, with great confidence we said, "OK, let's talk about the route...wasn't it beautiful?"

Most heads nodded in agreement. Even a few oohs and ahhs went up from the assembly of shop and home owners on the route, check-point workers, safety guards, food providers, teachers and sponsors assembled to give us feedback on our effort.

One participant remained quiet, making a slight grimace that signaled a differing opinion. We asked him if he had something to say and hesitantly at first, then elaborating as he went on, he said, *"Well, yes, it was pretty, and the beach is great most times, but it was awful hard walking the last half mile, because it was UP HILL!....and by the way, couldn't you have given us some place in the shade to walk at the end....we were so sunburned and it was the hottest part of the day."*

We sat with our mouths open. None of us had thought about the poor foot-weary walkers who we forced to trek *up hill* from the beach to the final check point! Aching muscles, sunburned body and blistered feet were not helped by having to fight the direct sun of mid-day along a shadeless beach the last 10% of the route! It should have been obvious, but it wasn't and it took a walker to point it out, because he had experienced it. Truly, he was an expert!

And, by the way, that *expert* was just 12 years old!

From then on, we involved walkers on our route planning committee, and let them be the expert leader when it came time to decide on a walk route. The role of leader shifted to home and shop owners living along the planned path when it came time to talk about how best to protect property as 10,000 walkers went by........and to the police representative when we were talking about safety.......and to former check point workers when we were deciding what supplies and locations to have for check points....and a nurse when we were talking about what to suggest walkers wear on their feet for the trek and what medical supplies and help we needed for walk day.....and on and on....

All of this demonstrates a new attitude and philosophy for leading volunteer efforts through **"Leadershift"**..when the leadership *shifts* to the person who has the best perspective of any part of a planned action.

Leadershift is not a rigid, "management du jour" fad, but a philosophy that allows for the flexibility of moving people from circle to circle, which are logically designed around specific work assignments. The design of these various work circles can differ from group to group depending on common-sense needs; the form is actually in direct response to the functional needs of the group.

Using Leadershift, **management charts** with neat rows of little boxes binding people and work to stagnant assignments are **replaced** by charts drawn in pencil and resembling maps of the galaxy or sketch pads of mad scientists, with arrows and dotted lines of connection very vexing to left-brained managers!

Leadershift replaces old patterns of static groups of people working on assignments regardless of their interests, skills or relationship to the work goal and instead institutes a form of leadership to meet today's demands for quality, fast response to needs and what many authors are calling the "age of the individual".

RELATIONAL MANAGEMENT

Leadershift also demands a new view of management that has little to do with directing nuts and bolts but has more to do with how people relate to work, themselves and others. Part of the job volunteer administrators will have in the next decade is delegation of work assignments to those who have a stake in the results, can work well with others assigned the task and feel confident enough within themselves to give the best effort possible.

I've named this new perspective to carry out work, "Relational Management", which I define as the working relationship between people and the process, work, mission and others.

Relational management offers what many new management gurus list as the key ingredients for success: an ability to be....

☞ *FAST.......FRIENDLY......FLEXIBLE........FOCUSED*

This style of management cares about Relationships (one of the 3 Rs governing all we do..along with Resources and Responsibilities) between people and clients, co-workers, governance, work, mission, wellness, demands, time, available energy, etc. etc. Like a game of chess, Relational Management seeks to constantly assess and attend to the best possible relationships that will ultimately lead to the mission; always thinking 10 steps ahead and willing to revise strategy at every move to attain the best results with the least amount of energy and/or problems.

Within its definition you may recognize the highly touted "Total Quality Management" of W. Edward Demming, brought down to the grassroots level, and made practical for the volunteer program executive of the real world. Possibly its greatest strength when joined to Leadershift, is its ability to adapt any of the management theories when called for.

Frequently organizations are finding that not every fad that is touted as the answer to all management, production or crisis concerns works for them. What they need more than "the one, true answer" is a wide range of options that can be held under the flexible umbrella of Relational Management and Leadershift

RELATIONAL MANAGEMENT DRESSED
IN DIFFERENT CLOTHES

What I call "Relational Management" is popping up under different labels but echoing the same concept......

In an April 1993 cover story in INC magazine, *"A Company of Business People"*, author John Case described companies which, by trial and error, have found paths away from management practices of the past 20 years.

The concept they have all arrived at by different routes, is to have everyone think like an owner. In this setting *"CEOs are freed up since responsibility for the business is no longer all at the top; managers don't have to figure out how to motivate lethargic employees; workers don't sit around waiting for instructions."* These words also describe what can happen under Relational Management.

More and more companies have come to realize that the old ways of working with people, developed to answer needs of the industrial society, no longer work. In that industrial setting efficiency ruled and called for interchangeable employees rather than skilled workers who were hard to replace.

From the need for such interchangeable employees arose two basic assumptions about work and workers:

> 1. Jobs must be defined as narrowly as possible.

> 2. Workers need close, direct supervision.

These two assumptions were carried over into the field of volunteer management, as volunteer leaders brought their business philosophy to the volunteer setting.

Specialists among volunteers were rarely recruited or encouraged in the early years of the 20th century. Interchangeable workers represented a philosophy in the field that translated into volunteers being shown how to do a particular work assignment (back to the bandage-rolling example!) as a group, thereby allowing their manager to call on any of them at any time to do the work.

This philosophy also typically placed volunteers in only non-essential jobs, so that they might be used to mind the children in a therapeutic day care center while teachers ate lunch, but were never used to actually _teach_ or work with the children. (An actual example!)

As management principles were translated to our unique needs in volunteerism in the 1960s and 70s, the emphasis shifted to greater attention of volunteer needs and ways to effectively manage their work. This sophistication in how we did business began, however, to be stretched beyond its limits as needs became more specialized, less generalized and more complex during the 80s and 90s.

Now, many decades after women first gathered to roll bandages or mind children, we find hospitals needing volunteers to provide a diversity of services from one-on-one patient counseling (i.e.: the "Why Me?" group of women with mastectomies) to victim support groups, parent-mentors for abuse-risk teen parents, gift shop managers, emergency room crisis volunteers, computer technicians, PR specialists to work on a recruitment campaign, etc.

The switch to such a variety of demands reflects societies shift to a specialization and niche focus and a hunger for anything customized. Recruitment has been made more difficult as volunteer directors identify needs that require very specific matches between work and worker.

It also demands a new, closer working relationship between the paid staff person who supervises the work and the volunteer as they work side by side to accomplish goals....again, it's Relational Management at work.

Where before the volunteer administrator directed the work of volunteers, now the need is for the volunteer to be managed by staff specialists who have the skills to insure quality work. The volunteer program executive then steps into the role of facilitator of the relationship between volunteer and work supervisor.

The volunteer administrator therefore, turns her attention to the relationship between volunteers, supervising staff, work and clients and helps to insure that the systems that surround those relationships empower rather than impede them.

This shift to Relational Management, rather than *worker* or *work* management... reflects what author Case details in his article as companies empower employees to work productively with one another.

It also mirrors the shift toward involving workers in decisions that effect them which is coming to be more prevalent in our field, and the breakdown of the old "we-they", adversarial relationships so obvious in the history of organizations which constantly refers to "management versus labor" or "volunteers versus staff".

In Relational Management, workers, paid, non-paid or stipended, are bound together to work on a common vision by trust and partnering while the volunteer administrator monitors the process to insure integrity and progress toward the mission, without trying to strictly control every little aspect.

Think about that.

There are many people who have great difficulty letting go of control and stepping instead into such a trust arrangement that is based on the positive assumptions that everyone involved is dedicated to the mission, willing to do their work and able to interact cooperatively with other workers regardless of position. There are those who talk about their belief in collaborative relationships but when push comes to shove, cannot really participate in them. Letting go often seems to be more difficult for some people than taking control!

One of the greatest measurements of the maturity of volunteerism will, I believe, come when we see volunteer program executives reach out beyond the confines of Management by Objectives (MBO) to embrace empowering trust relationships which resist "we-they" mentality, unrealistic demands on the manager and an insistence on compliant workers.

In a climate where trusted and clear relationships are nurtured and valued, innovation is possible as challenges emerge to provide services better, faster and at less cost.

Relational Management: caring..stimulating...trusting...effective and partnering, and responsive to the trends that are now defining our society.

190

CHANGING ROLES

The volunteer program executive of the year 2000 will see many changes in roles and responsibilities in comparison to the late 80's and early 90's.

The major change, which will overshadow and effect all other nuances of work, will be the role the volunteer program executive has in his or her organization.

In their book *Essential Volunteer Management*, authors Steve McCurley and Rich Lynch offer a graphic which shows how the roles have changed from a linear one between the volunteers and the volunteer director.....

Volunteer Director _____ Volunteers

• to a triangular relationship between the DVS, volunteers and supervising staff....

An example for this is within the description of how the Volunteer Department of the Courage Center changed to integrate volunteers throughout the entire system at the Center.

Another example comes from a dear friend, and one of the finest volunteer professionals in the country, Betty Greer at Rex Hospital in Raleigh, NC. Recently she was relating her experience in establishing a new program within the hospital where volunteers might serve in a new and innovative fashion. She shared that rather than going to the staff person involved and dropping a detailed plan on how to involve volunteers in the mission of that department, she instead planted the seed of the vision of how the work being done might be enhanced if volunteer-power was available to the staff.

She then shared the idea with the person who could make the decision to include or not include volunteers, along with the direct supervisors who would manage the volunteer's activities. After almost a year's incubation, the decision-maker asked for Betty's help to design volunteer job descriptions that would facilitate the inclusion of volunteers in the workings of the department.

By taking this patient, foundation-building approach, the program is almost guaranteed success as the paid staff had enough time and increasing faith to believe that volunteers can help. It was "their idea" and before one volunteer is ever put in place, the staff who must interact daily with volunteers **they select and place** (not Betty, please note!) has already made the commitment to the concept of non-paid staff working side by side harmoniously with paid staff.

Obviously the success of such a triangular relationship must be based on trust developed by the volunteer coordinator and the staff, which does not come overnight or easily. In switching to such a focus that avoids one volunteer coordinator trying to manage every volunteer work assignment in a large organization, many have found great apprehension and confusion in the minds of paid staff used to the more traditional relationship with volunteers _through_ the volunteer director.

A subtle resistance to change is taking place in the minds of such staff people, and it is the wise volunteer program executive who is forthright in addressing concerns that the paid staff, or even they themselves, may have:

- A fear of loss of too much responsibility as staff monitor work rather than relying on a volunteer administrator to do so.

- A fear of diminished quality of service by involving volunteers in areas where they have never worked before. Often staff see volunteers as unprofessional as much as non-professional.

- A fear that volunteers will be unreliable.

- A fear of increased liability exposure by involving volunteers.

192

- A perception that volunteers will increase rather than decrease work load.

- A fear that volunteers might take jobs away from employees.

- A belief that managing paid workers and volunteers is totally different, and that staff will not have the expertise needed to supervise volunteers.

- A confusion as to the volunteer program executive's role.

McCurley and Lynch offer some sound advice to directors of volunteers who express such concerns when they share:

> *"The role of the volunteer manager is to determine the concerns of the staff and then turn these concerns into a sense of confidence among the staff that the volunteers will be a useful addition to the agency.*

> In general, this means imparting two feelings to staff:

> A sense of benefit greater than the difficulties
> A feeling of control.....*"

To this statement by McCurley and Lynch, I would add the comments from Betty Greer, who further listed benefits that volunteers might bring to their work:

1. Giving staff time to dream.
2. Decreasing paid staff stress.
3. Opening avenues into places not readily available.
4. Volunteers having the time for little unessential things that mean so much to clients.
5. Improved staff morale, if work is done well.

INTERNAL CONSULTANCY

The role that volunteer directors of the future will adopt can best be described as "Internal Consultant".

In increasing numbers, directors of volunteers will be called on to be resources to others. This will force them into roles as internal consultants, who are called on to assess needs, suggest responses and offer options for assistance to remediate problems. More and more we will need to hone our consultancy skills so that we can in effect influence outcomes which we cannot manage.

Remember that a consultant is one who assists when called upon but rarely has the authority or responsibility to carry out the suggestions they offer. They can design systems but usually not implement them; they can suggest plans of action but rarely direct them as they unfold.

Strong volunteer program executives, such as the examples of Mary Wiser and Betty Greer, understand that they can see a place that volunteers could help a department, plant the seed of an idea of how they might be useful and respond to staff's acceptance of their integration and even assist in job designs, systems, etc. to implement the integration, but cannot actually MANAGE the volunteers directly.

This in effect causes the volunteer professional to juggle two roles simultaneously....that of working to initiate new integration of volunteers into existing work systems while also attending to on-going relationships between staff and volunteers that are already established. In the first scenario the relationship is linear between the director of volunteers and the staff as volunteer involvement is explored and designed, and in the second scenario, the relationship follows the triangular pattern suggested by McCurley and Lynch.

CONSULTANT SKILLS

The necessary consultant skills that will be required of such directors of volunteers include:

1. An ability to diagnose ways in which volunteers might help the goal of a department.
2. Reaching an agreement on how volunteers could help.
3. Assisting the staff in designing the organizational actions or systems needed.

Changing Roles of Volunteer Program Executives

Keep in mind that if volunteers cause more work than they alleviate, they will be thought of negatively. Design the management of the volunteer's work as simply and directly as possible through logical staff supervision.

Such a consultant role also demands checking back periodically to see how the systems, which looked so good on paper, are really working and then fine-tuning for any needed adjustments.

It will be critical for staff in organizations to trust the consultant skills of the volunteer program executive, so that they know they will have their continuing support as work is carried out. Under this far-reaching umbrella of internal consultant are several nuances worth note:

☞ She or he will be in constant, caring contact with clients, volunteers, staff and hierarchy to insure first hand understanding of needs so that any obstacles that could impede progress can be removed. Quality and efficiency will be an obsession as the public, volunteers, clients or beneficiaries and governance's demand the best possible service and contacts with the general population.

☞ Team building skills will be a necessity. The volunteer professional will need to create, manage and nurture teams at every level, each and every day.

☞ In addition to needing specific volunteer management skills, the volunteer program executive will have to have proficiencies in consulting, communication, systems management, negotiation, delegation and empowerment. The old style of management will be replaced by participatory ways to run efforts and the volunteer program executive will need to adopt this new approach, using it within the wider ranks of the organization.

General trends in business and management that will effect the volunteer department include:

1. The gap between workers and management will shrink.

2. Systems will be decentralized and humanized.

3. Innovation will be a top priority.

4. Creativity will be recognized and honored.

5. Values will be a critical ingredient in all that we do.

6. Care for each other and our earth will flourish.

7. Giving back and helping the community will be a natural part of people's lives.

8. Recruiting will be easier in some respects because less time will need to be spent on convincing people of the worthiness of causes.

9. Sharing goods and services will be a part of life.

10. There will be a change in outlook from gloom to hope...a healing vision.*

(excerpts from "Popcorn Report", "Megatrends for Women")

☞ Leadership will be a highly valued skill that employers will demand from those people they hire to lead volunteer departments and those already having those responsibilities. Each will have to have the quality and skills Aburdene and Naisbitt identify in their book, Megatrends 2000:

"A LEADER is an individual who builds followership by ethical conduct and by creating an environment where the unique potential of individuals can be actualized."

Such leaders will have to understand and work with what these authors call the *"first principle of the new age movement....the doctrine of individual responsibility"*. They define this as an ethical philosophy that states that the individual is a knowing participant in everything around them, even on a global level. It embraces an awareness that every person is connected to every other and that the rain-forests and the whales and starving children of Africa are not some removed concern on the nightly news, but interconnected with their own existence.

196

This age of the individual is a theme that runs through almost every futurists or trend-noter's work as each share examples that people are more in tune with the possibilities within themselves.

One such reporter, Bill Moyers, traveled the world over in search of answers regarding mind and body connections and found himself in China, observing an entire medical philosophy of "chi".....the body's own energy that pulsates internally but can be directed externally.

Moyers drew a connection between "chi" and the growing school of thought about how the great pyramids of Egypt were build, which states that the Egyptians somehow knew how to use their own psychic energy to levitate blocks of granite weighing up to 60 tons, to place them more easily in the structures that were over 500 feet in height!

All of this may have you whistling the theme from "Twilight Zone", but they are examples of the exploration of human energies. Lest you scoff too loudly, consider what singular and combined energies of individuals have done over the past few years as Communism fell, Eastern Europe realigned itself, the Berlin Wall came down, ecological concerns were addressed, drunk driving laws were tightened, and all manner of reforms....in education, health care, environment, politics, etc., came about in spite of the nay-sayers and skeptics that said none of it could be done.

 The age of the individual, conversely, empowers people to form closer alliances and build communities of like-minded people. It allows people to use technology to tailor their work to their life-style. Naisbitt and Aburdene, for example, work and live in a tiny town in Colorado, using the computer, fax, quick-mail and electronic equipment to keep them in touch with editors, fellow writers, and trend-compilation centers around the world.

For many years, I have shared a partnership with Steve McCurley that would not have been possible before the age of technology. With my office in my home near Chicago and Steve living in Olympia, Washington, we are in constant contact via phone, fax and express mail. We also have no formal contract between us, (a fact my attorney insists can't possibly be true), as we work as "individuals partnering" rather than a legal, hide-binding "partnership".

In our work together we have initiated several "partnering" arrangements with other, like-minded leaders who understand that working together in one area of our lives does not mean having to work together in all aspects. For example, we write our newsletter for the field of volunteerism, "GRAPEVINE" at our two offices. I then send my copy to Steve in Olympia on a computer disc or by Fax which then dumps it into his computer.

He then pulls it up on his screen, adds his copy, and those of contributing writers, edits and sets all 16 pages, including art work, design and layout, putting it into a camera-ready format. This is then sent by overnight express to Sacramento, CA where the volunteer office for sales of the CA. Ass'n of Hospitals and Health Systems (the folks that produce so many great recognition gifts & products) have it printed, processed and mailed to Grapevine readers around the world. They also keep all the records for subscriptions and renewals and thereby allow the newsletter to continue by taking over what had become an overwhelming chore for my small office to handle.

The test of good working relationships is always whether everyone involved feels as though they have a "win-win" situation. For Grapevine, we all feel that we each have the best end of the deal....Steve and I because we do not have to invest in personnel, larger equipment and more expensive software to process Grapeviner subscription data and the CAHHS because they do not have to create the original product. Along the vine, contributors such as Ivan Scheier, who provides his DOVIA (Directors of Volunteers in Agencies) Newsletter copy for inclusion in each issue of Grapevine, also feel they have a great thing going! Everybody wins.

As volunteer program executives are challenged to adapt to the age of the individual, they will be called on to design similar creative solutions to needs that different volunteers and assignments present. Some, in our profession, will not be able to muster enough flexibility or openness to new approaches, and will most likely have to find employment elsewhere, but most WILL adapt, finding a surprising number of options to help volunteers contribute to the mission of the organization.

Changing Roles of Volunteer Program Executives

☞ In the end, the leaders who will be the most effective in the 21st century will be those that understand their role as "Goal Tender", one who keeps their own and everyone else's eyes on which goals need to be realized.   Ones who accept that there are many roads to the same destination and are willing to select those which are the most efficient in terms of energy, time and resource expenditure.

A major trend that will impact all that we do for many years to come, and is part of goal-tending, is the focus on the consumer.   In volunteerism this means either the specific client or recipient of services or the general public who benefits from an organization's efforts.

Rather than turning to operations manuals and management textbooks, the driving force of many programs will become the continual questioning of "How can we best serve our consumer?" Instead of setting up rigid systems that are expected to work for everything, we will see systems set up in response to needs.   The old adage from architectural school of "Form follows Function" which means that how it is put together, its _"form"_, is dictated by what it is supposed to do, its _"function,"_ will guide us.

We will see an emphasis on our missions, a clarification and exporting of what it is we are about, so that everyone involved is directed toward the same goal.   People will choose their involvements by what mission drives them.   They will jump from effort to effort as they choose different approaches to the same driving concerns.

Parents will become active in a variety of efforts that they believe will impact their children positively; environmentalists will support many different activities that help our planet; activists will emerge in every variety of concerns and causes, and will work diligently to find new solutions to old problems.   In every case, one underlying principle will govern energies and involvement: "will the consumer (child, world's population, client, etc.) be best served by this activity?   Will the efforts really make a difference?   Is my energy best spent here to impact my concern?   Is the work meaningful to those served?"

☞ _In the years ahead, directors of volunteers will continually be called to task by volunteers acting as vigilantes, who demand that the end result of every action be service to the mission!_

199

Megatrends & Volunteerism

☞ Many volunteer administrators who work within a larger institution such as a hospital, college, museum, etc. will find that they may be asked to form a partnership with the director of development to raise moneys for the institution.

Many CEOs have noted the Gallup Poll statistic that says that volunteers traditionally donate twice what "non-volunteers" give to charity. They wish to leverage this revelation in several ways. First, some of them are asking for lists of volunteers in the hope that a direct appeal to those who already are involved with the work of the organization can be persuaded to also give money or goods in addition to their time and energy contributions.

This will cause an ethical dilemma for many volunteer program executives and possibly even some legal tugs of war. Who owns the list of volunteers? Who has access to it? How can it be used? How might it be abused? How does privacy figure into such considerations, especially when we are talking about self-help groups? To whom does the volunteer administrator have final responsibility....the agency, the CEO, the volunteers or clients? In this age of information, just where are the boundaries?

CEOs of groups are also sensitive to the trends we are talking about in this book and see that we are entering an age of humanness.

> **"The most exciting breakthroughs of the 21st century will occur not because of technology but because of an expanding concept of what it means to be human."**
> ....Megatrends 2000. Naisbitt & Aburdene

With this in mind, CEOs are realizing that their funding and support appeals need to be framed in the most human of terms, and that no one in the organization has better stories and examples of making a difference in the lives of clients and service recipients than the director of volunteers.

In one health care facility I know of, the directors of development and volunteers approached potential donors as a team, giving testimony to needs of clients as well as specific figures and identifying accountability factors of the hospital. Where the volunteer program executive provided human interest stories involving interactions between staff, volunteers and clients, the DD offered spread sheets, budget projections and proof of efficient use of donor dollars. When the development officer expressed a need of a specific amount or piece of equipment, the volunteer director gave human meaning to the request in terms of who would be helped by either.

It was a powerful duo, doubling the donations from the year before and creating lasting and productive relationships (there's that driving force again!) between the donor and the client through the vehicle of the institution. I expect us to see such partnering patterns in the future with many variations on the theme as people expand their definitions of the role of volunteer administrators.

☞ In addition to the volunteer administrator's role as primary consultant to staff for integration of volunteers throughout the organization, a second form of consultant role will emerge within very large organizations where individuals with very specific skills (conflict resolution, organization, personnel management, training, etc.) will be called on to offer those skills to others within the structure WHETHER OR NOT THE REQUEST HAS ANYTHING TO DO WITH VOLUNTEERS.

This will be a real departure for many current volunteer program executives, but they will need to be flexible and open enough to accept this change. Some, for example, who have demonstrated a high degree of expertise as a trainer may be called on to give a day long seminar on training to all the other department heads so that they in turn, might train their staff more effectively. When this happens, do not see it as something removed from your primary role as volunteer services executive......instead consider ALL that you do to interact positively and gain new respect from your peers throughout the entire organization as more building blocks for the credibility and relationships you and your department have with everyone else.

☞ A third variation on the theme of volunteer program executives as consultants, will be those who live in small communities where several agencies desire, but cannot fund, professional volunteer administrators. In such instances, one person, equipped with the necessary skills of volunteer management, leadership and consultantcy, may elect to contract with several groups to provide each with the guidance for an organized effort to incorporate volunteers.

Contracts will need to be carefully crafted and escape clauses will need to be available should any one of the agencies begin to demand more from the DVS than is realistic....a strong possibility since most agency directors have little understanding of what it takes to establish and maintain a good volunteer department.

Compensations should be generous as these consultants juggle the demands and needs of several groups.....a more difficult task than a single focus would present. I believe we will see more of this form of volunteer consultant in smaller communities or rural areas who offer a great deal of creativity as they put the pieces of their work together. One such consultant might have compensation from two groups and a permanent office & health benefits from a third. By-the-hour rates may be offered by one, by-assignment from another and a daily rate by a third.   Options are endless and can and will be explored by people and groups "partnering" innovatively to attain shared goals. It will be fun to watch!

☞ In addition to all of the preceding roles and skills volunteer administrators will be expected to master, there is a long list of subtle nuances that they will have to absorb as they accomplish their mission of systems design to empower volunteers and staff to work harmoniously.

Here is simply a laundry list I hope won't drive you to drink or a career change!

Coach	*Systems Manager*	*Partner: $$*
Resource	*Flexible Agent*	*People Link*
Manager	*Capacity Assessor*	*Melder*
Counselor	*Change Agent*	*Professional*
Mobilizor	*Information Gleaner*	*Goal Tender*
Strategizor	*Integrity Auditor*	*Reality-check*

Changing Roles of Volunteer Program Executives

Advocate	*Leader*	*Ombudsman*
Evaluator	*Simplifier*	*Political Pro*
Collaborator	*Consultant*	*Resource Coordinator*
Mediator	*Influencer of Influencers*	

........and Still Able to Leap Tall Buildings in a Single Bound!

OVERCOMING RESISTANCE TO CHANGE

Many of the roles that the volunteer program executive will take on in the years ahead will have to deal with change and people's reaction to it. As shifts are made in the work patterns within organizations, those most dramatically affected ....volunteers & paid staff..... will most probably demonstrate some resistance to altering "the way we've always done it."

The wise volunteer administrator, therefore, will simply build in sensitivity to the issue of change and people's fears surrounding it, helping everyone to adjust to new patterns and relationships in work circles.

There are nine areas of change that foster resistance in workers, whether they are paid or non-paid, full-time or part-time, that volunteer program executives should be aware of:

1. *Changes that are perceived to lower prestige or status:* You might want to prepare for some of the volunteers feeling that being supervised directly by paid staff members is somehow 'lower' in prestige than being supervised by yourself as head of a department. To reduce or eliminate this resistance:

   a. Discuss the perception of the change with those affected as you plan for it.
   b. Insure everyone understands the real need for change .
   c. Insure everyone understands there is nothing personal in the switch of supervisors.

2. _**Changes that cause fear:**_ There are always those people who simply fear any change in general and others who might fear changes you propose specifically. Keep in mind that change demands new information, rules, parameters, etc. and most of us are very comfortable with things as they are, because we already know how to deal with them. To reduce or eliminate this resistance:

    a. Examine any changes you are proposing that might harbor fears.
    b. Ask those people who will be affected by the change to provide input.
    c. Discuss these fears openly, helping people lay aside unfounded fears.
    d. Discuss options of response to real fears that are expressed.
    e. Help people feel a sense of control in the changes...loss of control is a base of fear.

3. _**Changes that effect job content or tangible rewards:**_ Paid staff may dig in their heels upon hearing that they may have to work in a more direct relationship with volunteers. This will change their work pattern, and to over-worked staff, the addition of volunteers may look more like **adding** to this load rather than helping to **relieve** it!

Volunteers too, will resist changes that alter their work relationships. Someone familiar with their single-phone-line duties as a receptionist, for example, might find their knees going to jelly and 100 reasons why "it just won't work!" when told they will have to learn a new 12-line, automated voice mail system!

Changing any reward tradition may bring you the shock of the year, as your sweetest, dearest volunteer turns into Connan the Barbarian in defense of the banquet, plaque or pin you propose altering!

To help reduce such opposition to proposed changes (and to prevent finding a crossbow arrow in your back!):

    a. Involve those to be affected in decisions, showing clearly-demonstrated needs.

    b. Involve them in exploring options to meet needs.

    c. Create new avenues of rewards to substitute for any old that you change.

4. *Changes that reduce authority or freedom of acting:* Changes in this category feel like a demotion to people and need to be clearly understood and perceived as necessary before they are implemented. To reduce this resistance:

    a. Articulate the reasons why the change is necessary....systems simplification, etc.

    b. Insure that you are not changing a whole system simply to control a troublesome individual! Never over-react to one person's inappropriate behavior, trying to create rules that might put him "back in line" and which others really do not need.

5. *Changes that disrupt established work routines:* This obviously is the territory you will be entering as you shift responsibility from direct management to others in the organization. You will be disrupting "comfort" zones and will have to contend with one of the major considerations trend-watchers note about people today: they want to feel **"safe"**. Once again, your job in eliminating this resistance is to produce evidence of a legitimate need for such a change, and to involve those affected in the planning stages of the change.

Be patient with this resistance. Keep in mind that you have probably been thinking about it for a long time, but others are still adjusting to it as new information and a new concept.

6. *Changes that rearrange formal and informal group relationships:* In dealing with this resistance, you are again treading on an area trend-watchers see as super-critical to Americans today: **Relationships.** Any effort to change relationships, by putting together new work groups, shifting people into new departments, supervision by someone new to them, etc. will meet with considerable resistance unless presented carefully. To lower this response:

    a. Introduce changes slowly.

    b. Employ the help of an 'authenticator' or trusted leader

    who is firmly established within the group to help you introduce the change at an appropriate pace and time.

    c. Be sensitive to people who feel less trustful of the new relationships created.

    d. Insure that any new people introduced into a group do not become the brunt of anger by others already there regarding the change.

    e. Help those affected understand that the change is not directed personally at anyone.

7. _Changes that are forced without explanation or worker participation:_ In spite of popular thinking, people really do not like surprises, especially when they pop up around familiar turf such as the work place. This is one of the most common errors made in dealing with change and it sets up a potential conflict between those who resent the forced and unexpected change and those who imposed it because it seemed so logical and needed.

Neither adults nor children like to be forced into anything. When persuaded, they follow willingly, even passionately, but when forced, they drag their feet, withholding their support and cooperation.

At all costs, try to avoid forcing an unexpected change, and if one is forced on you that you have to pass along to others, negotiate a plan with your higher-ups to involve those affected and create a sensitive timeline of enforcement.

Keep people abreast of future plans and options, remembering the sage saying:

        "What I am not UP on, I will be DOWN on."

8. _Changes that are resisted because of mental or physical exhaustion:_ Change requires hard work in most cases. Keep in mind that if people are physically or mentally exhausted, the work can seem to be even more formidable than it really is, and resistance will heighten. Look for such resistance when you are in the middle of or just finished with a major event, during the holiday seasons, at the time of another major change, when key individuals are under great personal stress or are ill, or when there are extreme outside pressures (the 1991 Persian Gulf War created such tension in Americans that wise groups postponed scheduled changes and efforts until it was over).

Scheduling is the key answer to reducing such resistance. Plan everything you do in pencil, being willing to change to more appropriate and productive timing. If you simply do not have that option, talk openly with influential people in the groups affected about your inability to shift the timing, and your need to have them help you make the changes positively.

9. **_Changes that surround symbolic issues:_** In another section of this book, I speak at length about the Theory of Significance that drives people to protect that which they see as connected to their personal significance. It is often called the "Founder Syndrome" when it produces resistance to change in an effort "owned" by the resistor. The issue of symbolism is a variation on that theme.

Most groups consciously or unconsciously develop symbols of their existence. In hospitals the symbol is often a uniform; in large organizations, specific rewards such as "outstanding volunteer of the year" designation; in many groups it is a logo, name or slogan etc.

To avoid the flash-points of such symbolism and reduce resistance to change surrounding them:

    a. Identify symbolic areas, efforts and items in your organization.
    b. Know your group's history... that elderly volunteer who seems to be around a lot may be the originator of the program you've suggested changing.... no wonder she rose up with a hatchet in her hand upon hearing your idea!
    c. Tread carefully when thinking of changing something in a group. Does it really need changing? Are you simply imposing your personal preference? Does keeping it the way it is harmful? Are the benefits worth the cost of the change?

It is critical for the volunteer service executive..... especially one entering a new position in an established organization, to understand these nine potential danger zones of resistance. By being sensitive to the potential for opposition to proposed changes, you will be able to deal effectively and non-defensively to reduce resistance.

Remember that you are frequently asking those affected to **not** take the change personally. You, in turn, must not take any resistance personally either!

If you are hoping that those involved will see the need for change and suggest it themselves (thereby owning the change), you might try an exercise I proposed in my writing, _"Overcoming Resistance to Change"_:

Establish a time and setting where people can gather in a relaxed atmosphere, such as a day-long retreat or brain-storming time, where people can think about the future. Then ask that they answer the following questions first in writing as individuals, then assembling in groups to discuss common responses and insights:

May be don't need to.............anymore.

Maybe we do need to..............some more.

Maybe we need to.................some time soon.

Maybe we need to .... once again.

Maybe we need to .... sometimes.

I remember that once we had the idea to .... but we decided against it. Maybe we need to look at it again.

I recall a feeling we once had in our work setting that was really great! It was................. and I think we need to figure out how to get it back.

What if we ....

Such an exercise, especially if you tailor it to your own group, will probably spark some great dialogue to suggest creative and innovative new ideas and allow some existing efforts to be eased out and replaced by new ones.

The only caution I would add over such a meeting is, don't schedule it if you have no intention of really listening to people's concerns, ideas and feelings! Folks are smart enough to catch on to insincere requests for creative thinking, and with their time and energy at a premium, chances are you would lose a whole lot of volunteers around such subterfuge and a ton of credibility with paid staff.

In assisting people to move beyond their resistance to changes, several rules of thumb can help you in this process. Be sure you:

1. Identify the root cause of the resistance.
2. Involve people in decisions that effect them.
3. Make sure the change is really needed.
4. Understand all change produces adjustment and feelings of loss.
5. Help people envision the end result when change is implemented.
6. Be very clear about what position people will have when the change is a reality.
7. Enlist key influencers to assist in garnering the support of others.
8. Avoid change during high stress times if possible.
9. Remember that feelings are facts. Be sensitive to how people feel about change.
10. Disclose as much background information as possible in sharing why change is needed.
11. Be clear as to expectations.
12. Do everything you can to gain and be worthy of people's trust.
13. Openly reward those who help facilitate the change.

....and one last bit of advice......

14. **NEVER PROMISE WHAT YOU CAN'T DELIVER!**

SOCIAL CHANGE

The volunteer program executive of today and the future will be working against a backdrop of major social change.

These changes point the way toward a growing activism that particularly affects women who, Aburdene and Naisbitt tell us, *"are trading in their old roles as under appreciated volunteers to serve as* _activists in African American, Hispanic and Asian communities. They are also reinventing volunteering by compelling charitable organizations to offer people meaningful work and time schedules working people can handle."_

Because of this shift, volunteer program executives will be working with a different work force and have to adapt to it's changing characteristics.

The guiding principles of successful social change will need to be recognized by volunteer administrators as they try to understand and assimilate volunteers coming from these new perspectives of:

Old Thinking of....	**to**	**New Thinking of:**
Win/lose		_Win/win (the social entrepreneur)_
Top down		_Grassroots (self-sufficient independence)_
"Politically correct "		_What works fairly (form follows function)_
Educational bureaucracy		_Choice (a revolution of information)_
Victims		_Advocates (addressing terrible issues)_
Government/government aid		_Investing in entrepreneurs (fostering self-reliance)_

REINVENTING VOLUNTEERING

The new thinking outlined above, along with the megatrends that impact volunteerism, will create a demand for change in how we view, define, relate to and enlist volunteers and ultimately how volunteer program executives will need to redefine their work.

Let me list some of the changes in volunteering I see on the horizon as suggested by the trends that swirl around us.

Volunteering and its leaders will need to....
- be "time" sensitive, wasting none of this precious resource.
- accommodate full-time workers or school schedules.

210

- be flexible.
- offer meaningful work.
- drop out-moded efforts or unnecessary work.
- address real issues rather than imaginary ones.
- respect other demands volunteers carry.
- design systems that empower rather than impede.
- reduce or eliminate red tape.
- explain expectations carefully and honestly.
- offer opportunities for creativity.
- afford a safe climate in which to work.
- respect individual differences.
- acknowledge diversity without letting it divide.
- see the work place as a major connecting point for volunteers.
- involve seniors appropriately.
- reject assumptions.
- share knowledge openly.
- let volunteers leave.
- recognize qualitatively as well as quantitatively.
- see efforts globally.
- customize work and rewards.
- balance wellness with work.
- entertain fun and playfulness.
- offer skill building.
- see education as a partner in community service.
- build coalitions and collaborations.
- refuse to reinvent the wheel.
- address unmet needs; refuse to duplicate.
- constantly seek improvement.
- accept criticism and explore it for growth opportunities.
- reject any tyranny of the prominent.
- be ethical and accountable.
- build relationships and community.
- expend resources wisely.
- understand that human energy is in shorter supply; use it wisely.
- think ecologically; conserve the planet and its' people!
- be mission focused.
- drop things that don't work or make sense.
- reframe problems as challenges.
- stop when finished; know when to quit.

The list could go on endlessly, but these come to mind after examining trends around us, and in fact have all been addressed in the previous nine chapters of this book. Actually, it might be a great starting point for any volunteer group to begin a customized list of its own regarding the characteristics needed to survive and THRIVE in the modern world!

THE VOLUNTEER PROGRAM EXECUTIVE AS DETECTIVE

The volunteer program executive or leader will need to be on the constant lookout for ideas and information outside of our field that can offer clues for us in our work.

Keep in mind that the McDonald breakfast concept was a flash of "ah-HA!" to an executive of that great company after reading an article in the paper documenting how many women were in the workforce. In his mind the connection between his company and that piece of demographic information was that with both adult partners in a relationship working, there was less time (or logic) for a wife and/or mother to fix breakfast. Therefore, why not offer an option from a trusted and well-located friend like McDonalds?

The rest, as they say, is history, and though we may all enjoy an occasional Egg McMuffin, the real learning in that tale is the transfer of seemingly unrelated data to the work of McDonalds.

As leaders, we will need to constantly play detective, rooting out possible linkages to our own work. Let me offer a little test right here and now to start you off.

A recent demographic study was done for the hotel industry to see what trends might tell us about what guests want/need in their relationship with a hotel. What might attract them? What might create a warm-feeling and therefore, allegiance to a hotel?

You will note that the research was already solidly entrenched in the understanding that people today want relationships with their supplier services. That same theme comes up again and again in advertising, when you hear that "Ford Motor Co. doesn't just build cars, they build relationships", or "You're still in good hands with Allstate" or "Chrysler products: a name you can trust".

The hotel study showed that in the early 1980s, people responded positively when there was a lot of "stuff" in their room.... shampoo, shower cap, soaps, mouth wash, toothpaste, robe, bathroom TV, etc. etc. No surprise that history now labels that era "the age of consumption".

In the mid to later 1980s, however, a subtle shift took place. People began to worry about such things as junk bonds, the soaring deficit, corporate raiding and take-overs, a decline in housing starts, but didn't want to voice their concern too loudly when everyone else seemed to be saying "all is wonderful!" and offer happy-talk in press conferences.

But worry they did, and so hotels began to offer in-room bars with alcohol and snacks, so those worry-warts could drown their concerns in Jim Beam or Snickers bars. The patrons of those hotels loved it and came back again and again!

Today, as "let's pretend" time in our history is over and people are actually finding out that things are not as good as we'd all been told, they are down right scared and expressing a need for reassurance that "everything's going to be all right".

How are hotels responding? With something I love.....

- an option for guests to order warm cookies and icy cold milk at a time of their choice!

Yes, old favorites of oatmeal, peanut butter, sugar or (my choice) chocolate chip cookies served warm with a cold glass of milk and placed at bedtime next to your turned-down bed....usually served by an older woman. An attempt to offer the world's oldest, number one security assurance, a "Mom"!

....To remind guests that this is a hotel where it is **safe**, where you can come and be **comforted**; where you can be warmly **welcomed**, taken care of and offered the wonderful foods of your youth (real or imagined). Mom.... Grandma..... Aunt Sadie or your favorite baby-sitter, Mrs. Lovecushion!

How does this apply to volunteer programs? You've already connected the dots and passed the test, I' m sure. The transfer of learning for a volunteer program, is that it needs to be safe.... physically, psychologically, spiritually; that volunteers must be assured of success, of enjoyable surroundings (in the sense of effectiveness, not necessarily comfort), of having warm relationships, of feeling they can return again and again and find the same, good feelings.

It's the "Mom" factor. And it will be with us for a long time.

THE ROLE OF VOLUNTEER PROGRAM EXECUTIVE AS AN ARMS-LENGTH DIRECTOR

One of the innovative solutions to help attract and keep excellent workers for companies is "flex-space", where people do their work from home with the aide of a FAX, modem and computer on-line hook ups.

The volunteer program executive will need to look at such options, plotting ways to incorporate the concept and manage such volunteers at arm's length, a different role for most.

I believe we will see growth in the at-home (or in-office), at-you-own-timing voluntary options of flex-space and also recognize a variety of creative ways to make such assignments productive. The principles of managing these options will be the same for all varieties of work:

1. Identify whole jobs or significant pieces of a larger effort which are transportable.

2. Identify those systems needed to enable the work to be done off-site.

3. Identify the materials and support needed to empower volunteers to accomplish the work.

4. Set instructions and time frames effecting the work and train volunteers accordingly.

5. Establish quality and accountability standards and share these with volunteers along with reporting procedures.

6. Create appropriate recognition systems.

With these steps as a basis, I can see a growing number of volunteer program executives designing creative work assignments for people who are willing to do projects off-site to conserve time, energy and physical demands of having to do work at the program site.

Such flexibility may encourage previously reluctant categories of people to become involved, including:

1. People home-bound because of physical limitations.

2. People with no transportation.

3. People who feel unsafe in leaving their home or coming to your site.

4. Those who do not have the extra time it would take to come to your location.

5. Those who prefer to do work at unorthodox times.

6. Young parents who can only do work around the changing schedules of small children in their own home.

7. Professionals with ever-changing work schedules such as Realtors.

8. People who have "down-time" at work and can do assignments sporadically in their work site, such as firemen, teachers, etc.

9. People whose volunteer assignments are connected to their paid work, such as graphic artists for whom it is simply more convenient to work in their office.

The list of assignments off-site workers could accomplish is only limited by imagination and might include:

Record keeping	Phoning	Event arrangements
Graphic arts/design	Supply ordering	Mailings
Newsletters	Research	Accounting
Creation of recognition items	Customer response	Child care
Correspondence	Statistics	Product development
Counseling	Order fulfillment	Mentoring
Data entry	Copy writing	Material creation

That should be enough to start you thinking!

VOLUNTEERISM AND THE CORPORATION

In her *"Popcorn Report"*, author Faith Popcorn spends a great deal of time pointing to a major trend of "niche-focusing", attention to a rather narrowly defined segment of the general public.

Creative examples abound in entrepreneurial efforts as new businesses are built around attention to a specific need or demographic:

- An Oklahoma couple offers their services as substitute Bed & Breakfast sitters, going in to take over the B & B when owners want to get away.

- A publisher offers a newsletter for parents and grandparents who want to help their children get more out of school.

- A retired industrial arts teacher offers "Santa's workshop" for parents who don't have the time or talent (or patience) to put together those toys packed in boxes with the innocent little statement: "Some Assembly Required" printed in blood on the side. He does the assembly for them and can barely breathe for all the work he has in the three months before Christmas!

The same trend will become more and more obvious in

volunteerism as specialists find a variety of niches with unique characteristics, including the most obvious...Corporations.

The corporate volunteer executive will act as a liaison between the community at large, the internal corporate community and its members.

In working with services to the company workers, she will have to have skills in assessment and planning as she audits needs within the corporate community and creates systems and efforts to meet those needs such as child and elder day-care, transportation, family and financial counseling, abuse prevention, personal mentoring, retirement planning, etc.

The corporation volunteer executive will also work closely with the highest levels of leadership to be able to design efforts that reflect the organization's commitment to servicing the community at large.

As if this were not enough to fill the corporate volunteer administrator's daily planner, she will also need to serve as a resource person for community agencies wishing to recruit volunteer workers for their group's efforts.

In general, corporations will more and more become centers for community agencies to approach to locate and interact with potential volunteers.

By the turn of the century, I believe we will see more creative methods of tapping the corporate community through:

1. Whole-company presentations, enabled by executive support, that educates workers to specific agencies/ missions, clientele, volunteer opportunities and needs.

2. Drop-in information or even "ads" in corporate newsletters for volunteer opportunities... a variation on the growing trend of "infomercials".

3. Cooperation in planning, establishing and managing pre-retirement seminars which steer workers toward volunteerism. (Statistics indicate that volunteering is good for one's health!)

4. Wellness training that includes suggestions for workers becoming involved in volunteer jobs that provide satisfaction and feelings of "making a difference".

In general, agency volunteer administrators will be very sensitive to the megatrend of relationship-building and work to do just that with as many people as possible. The corporation will provide an opportunity for volunteer recruiters to contact large numbers of people at a single stroke and of forging a relationship by tying into a corporate culture.

The corporation, for example, that manufactures child safety seats might be a target of an agency that provides safe houses and support for abused women and children.

Creativity and need will merge to form relationships where like-missions converge. The field of professional volunteer administration will benefit as more and more corporations see the wisdom of community involvement and want a specialist to handle such a challenge, and volunteer program executives will benefit as they have an identifiable corporate community with which to interact in various ways.

The corporate connection is upon us!

MANAGEMENT BY FACT

After having proposed that volunteer program executives will no longer be managing volunteers directly, but the **systems** that empower volunteers to be an invaluable part of attaining the mission of an organization, I still need to address the issue of direct management.

Obviously, you will need to manage work in your office and those people who do indeed answer directly to you. What you have learned in the past regarding the functions of management-plan, organize, staff, direct and assess, and their components-goal, objectives, plans of action, job designs, recruitment, interviewing, placing, training, supervising and evaluating- are just as valid today as they ever were.

218

You may even find yourself having to incorporate regulations imposed by outside control, such as new physical requirements for each job as imposed by OSHA and the Americans with Disabilities Act, etc.

Beyond just the technical or scientific edge to management, however, are the attitudes that are necessary to insure that management accomplishes the over-riding "spirit" of the effort.

A printed job description does not come to life until someone sits down with a prospective volunteer and works to have the job designed to meld the needs of the volunteer and the organization. It is the attitude of cooperation and shared commitment that is the **spirit** of the job design and makes the match of worker-to-work successful.

Management by Fact is the name I have given to a realistic attitude I believe the volunteer program executive of the future will need to keep in mind as she goes about her management job functions, and may include some new perspectives for us:

1. Recognition of a problem or appraisal of what is happening that could be improved.

2. Gathering data about the problem, honestly and realistically.

3. Designing counter-actions to solve problems or improve performance.

4. Testing the new actions for success, then standardizing the action for replication.

All of these steps are borrowed from the demand for total quality management, an effort sparked by the work of W. Edward Demming and clearly articulated in the writings of Philip Crosby (*"Quality is Free"* and *"Quality Without Tears"*) and Larry W. Kennedy (*"Quality Management in the Nonprofit World"*).

In looking at these action steps, we need to examine them further for the attitudes necessary to make them work. Without the

219

accompanying attitudes, the action is pre-determined to fail. I have become convinced of this as I worked with many groups who seemed to be going about doing the right things, yet the results were less than successful.

A deeper examination on my part uncovered right messages with wrong delivery methods such as a "sincere letter of thanks" written by a computer to a wrongly-spelled name; an incongruence between asking for input and having no system to utilize it; an expression of a desire to collaborate as equal partners but a demand for total control by one of the parties, etc. etc.

In using Management by Fact, specific actions demand a balance of the appropriate attitude:

1. Recognizing problems demands a realistic attitude that can challenge established patterns.

2. Gathering data requires openness, honesty and no sacred cows.

3. Designing a remedy requires creativity and innovation plus risk taking.

4. Testing for results demands patience, an ability to adjust and tinker with responses.

5. Applying learning from the tests into a new process requires flexibility, acceptance of change and an ability to see solutions as evolving, rather than pat.

All of these actions, and others you find necessary to your organizational systems and challenges, demand an openness to new thoughts......an ability to "go outside the lines" in your thinking to create forms that follow the needed functions.

All of this must be rooted in an attitude of honest inquiry to get factual information and then build on it to give us road maps to where we want to go, accepting the fact that the way may have to change as we define new destinations.

THE WINDING ROAD FOR VOLUNTEER PROGRAM EXECUTIVES

As we look to the future of volunteerism, I believe our roles will change into forms yet undreamed of as we focus on what needs to be done and then wisely shed the belief that there are only one or two paths to those ends.

- We will see the expansion of the "discipline" of volunteer management to embrace new skills of consultancy and Leadershift, and explore new dimensions with those who wish to stretch volunteerism to new heights and depths.......

- With our inherent nature of caring activism in tact, we will create a new revolution that sweeps the world with the only force strong enough and sensitive enough to bring hope to the hopeless and fulfill dreams thought to be lost.....

- We will stop managing volunteers directly and exclusively and focus on creating and maintaining systems that empower volunteers and others to reach their shared goals and vision.....

- And we will come to embrace a variety of diversities among our own ranks and from around our world, honoring them for the work they do and our shared mission of accomplishing miracles through the unique gifts people offer by giving of themselves freely to the betterment of others.

In short, we will change the world by setting the spirit, the tone and the vision of a new world order in terms of caring, sharing and building community; instead of only responding to trends, we will set them; instead of reacting to what already is, we will create the agendas for what can be when infused with the voluntary spirit.

Through the attitude of servant-leadership, our profession of volunteer administration will lead the way through the turmoil and violence of diverse demands to a spirit of community and shared commitment for a safer, healthier and mutually-supportive world.

Megatrends & Volunteerism

The road will not be an easy one.

It will have dead ends and false road signs, rocks and barriers, but we will find a way to endure and progress, fueled by the passion of our mission and strengthened by the fire of our concern for our companions on the trek.

And in our journey we will rediscover again, the spirit of volunteering.....the ultimate Megatrend our vision can bring about.

> *"Some see things as they are and ask, "Why?";*
> *I see things as they could be and say, "Why Not?"*

> ..Robert Kennedy, quoting G.B. Shaw

Bibliographic List of References Used

Books:

American Heritage Dictionary. 2nd College Edition. (Bantam, Doubleday, Dell) 1983.

Aburdene, Patricia & Naisbitt, John. *Megatrends 2000.* (Wm. Morrow & Co.) 1990.

Aburdene, Patricia & Naisbitt, John. *Megatrends for Women.* (Villard Books) 1992.

Barker, Joel Arthur. *Future Edge: Discovering the New Paradigms of Success.* (Wm. Morrow & Co.) 1992.

Bennis, Warren & Nanus, Burt. *Leaders: The Strategies for Taking Charge.* (Harper & Row) 1985.

Bryson, John & Crosby, Barbara. *Leadership for the Common Good.* (Jossey-Bass) 1992.

Byham, William. *Zapp! The Lightning of Empowerment.* (Harmony Books) 1988.

Courage Center. *Courage: The Story of the Courage Center.* (Courage Center) 1989.

Covey, Stephen. *Principle-Centered Leadership.* (Summit Books)1991.

Drucker, Peter. *Post-Capitalist Society.* (Harper Business) 1993.

Drucker, Peter. *The New Realities.* (Harper & Row) 1989.

Gardner, John. *Building Community.* (Independent Sector) 1991.

Garfield, Charles. *Peak Performers.* (Avon Books) 1986.

Glasser, William, M.D.. *Control Theory.* (Harper & Row) 1984.

Goodstein, Leonard, & Noland, Timothy, & Pfeiffer, J. Wm. *Shaping Your Organization's Future.* (Pfeiffer & Co.) 1993.

Hoff, Benjamin. *The Te of Piglet.* (Dutton Book) 1992.

James, Jennifer Ph.D. *Success is the Quality of the Journey.* (Newmarket Press) 1986 Rev.

Kennedy, Larry. *Quality Management in the Nonprofit World.* (Jossey-Bass) 1991.

Kouzes, James & Posner, Barry. *The Leadership Challenge.* (Jossey-Bass) 1987.

Lynch, Richard & Vineyard, Sue. *Secrets of Leadership.* (Heritage Arts) 1991.

Lynch, Richard. *Lead!* (Jossey-Bass) 1993.

McCurley, Stephen & Lynch, Richard. *Essential Volunteer Management.* (Heritage Arts) 1989.

Moore, Gail & MacKenzie, Marilyn. *Building Credibility With the Powers That Be.* (Heritage Arts) 1990.

Naisbitt, John. *Megatrends.* (Warner Books) 1982.

Naylor, Harriet. *Volunteers: Today.* (Dryden Associates) 1967.

O'Connell, Brian. *For Voluntary Organizations In Trouble Or Don't Want To Be.* (Independent Sector) 1993.

O'Connell, Brian & Knauft, E. B. *Financial Compensation in Nonprofit Organizations.* (Independent Sector) 1993.

Popcorn, Faith. *The Popcorn Report.* (Doubleday) 1991.

Sargent, Alice. *The Androgynous Manager.* (Amacom) 1981.

Scheier, Ivan Ph.D. *Exploring Volunteer Space.* (VOLUNTEER) 1980.

Toffler, Alvin. *Powershift.*

Vineyard, Sue. *Marketing Magic for Volunteer Programs.* (Heritage Arts) 1985.

Vineyard, Sue. *Beyond Banquets, Plaques & Pins: Creative Ways to Recognize Volunteers.* (Heritage Arts) 1989 Rev.

Vineyard, Sue. *Overcoming Risistance to Change.* (Heritage Arts) 1991.

Wyant, Susan & Brooks, Phyllis. *The Changing Role of Volunteerism.* (United Hospital Fund of NY) 1993.

Periodicals, Articles & Papers:

American Corporate Community Service; Fortune, Nov. 30, 1992.
Ben & Jerry's: Management with a Human Flavor; Robert Sonenclar, Hemispheres, Mar. 1993.

Beyond The Year 2000; multiple authors, Special Edition, Time, Fall 1992.
Brian O'Connell Considers Boards; The Connection, Volunteers in Action,
   Spring 1992.
Changing the Paradigm: The Second Report, Points of Light Foundation,
   June 1993.
Community Perspective, Quality Improvement Vital to Health Care Reform;
   Kim Chapin, The Reporter, Illinois Hospital Ass'n., Nov. 23, 1992.
A Company of Businesspeople; John Case, Inc., April 1993.
Contract Volunteer Services; Loyce Haran, Siobhan Kenney & Mark
   Vermillion; Leadership, Jan-Mar 1993.
Corporate Social Responsibility & Volunteerism: A Perfect Blend; Richard
   Eamer, NME Volunteer Spotlight, Spring 1992.
Decentralize, Yes, But Wait For The Right Moment; Tom Peters, Chicago
   Tribune, May 10, 1993.
Deming Still Produces the Quality of Belief; Ronald Yates, Chicago Tribune.
Fact Sheet on The International Alliance; Independent Sector, 1993.
Family Matters: The First Year; Points of Light Foundation 1992.
Family Values; Norval Glenn; American Demographics, June 1992.
Fashion Fits Firm, Tom Peters, Chicago Tribune, Oct. 18, 1992.
Female Values Could Rescue World, Swedish Sociologist Suggests; Chicago
   Tribune, May 16, 1993.
Gallup Poll on Volunteering & Giving: 1992; Independent Sector. Oct. 1992.
Harder Times Have Not Stunted American Charity; Charles Storch, Chicago
   Tribune, May 26, 1993.
Hospitals Take Lead in ADA Compliance, Education; Kim Chapin, The
   Reporter, Illinois Hospital Ass'n, Dec. 28, 1992.
Hot New Trends; Success, March 1990.
Knowledge the Wealth of Nations?; Storer Rowley, Chicago Tribune, May
   16, 1993.
LB Sponsors National Youth & Family Volunteerism Initiatives; Lutheran
   Brotherhood Bond, Summer 1993.
Managing the Baby Busters; Charlene M. Solomon, Managing Diversity
   newsletter, Nov. 1992.
Most Companies Encourage Volunteerism; Tracy Fine, Chronicle of
   Philanthropy, May 4, 1993.
*National Service Initiative Takes Shape With Boston's 'City Year" as One
   Model;* Mary Jordan, Washington Post, Dec. 13, 1992.
New Industrial Revolution Hits U.S. Big Business; Wm. Neikirk, Chicago
   Tribune, Feb.21, 1993.
No Shortcuts in Hunt for Community; David Warsh, Boston Globe/Chicago
   Tribune, May 23, 1993.
Nostradamus of Marketing; Karin Winegar; Minneapolis-St. Paul Star
   Tribune; Mar. 17, 1993.
Slow Going on National Service, Wm. Buckley Jr.; Chicago Tribune.
Taking Volunteerism Into the 21st Century; Maria Smith, Journal of
   Volunteer Administration, Fall 1989.

The Importance of Philanthropy & Voluntary Initiative; Independent Sector, April 1992.

The Leader As Servant; Walter Kiechel III, Fortune, May 4, 1992.

The Mentoring Relationship in Action; IUME Briefs, Aug. 1992.

The Nonprofits' Quiet Revolution; Peter Drucker, Leadership, 1989.

The Sleeping Giant of School Reform; Joe Nathan & Jim Kielsmeier, Phi Delta Kappan; June 1991.

To Stay the Communitarian Course; Amitai Etzioni, Communitarian Reporter, Fall 1992.

Teams/Coalitions/Volunteers; Gail Dobbs; The Safety Net. Dec. 1991.

Trends in Charitable Giving & Volunteerism; Frank Martinelli. Center for Public Skills Training.

A Vision for All; Leader in Action, Fall 1991.

Volunteer 2000 Study; American Red Cross. 1989.

Volunteerism Is Changing!; Eva Schindler-Rainman, Ph.D., Journal of Volunteer Administration, Summer 1990.

What's Ahead in the Decency Decade?, Solar Directions, Winter 1992.

Wounding the Gun Lobby; Richard Lacayo, Time, Mar. 29, 1993.

Young Volunteers in Action..What is It?; Education Connection, Volunteers in Action, Spring 1992.

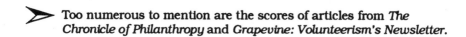 Too numerous to mention are the scores of articles from *The Chronicle of Philanthropy* and *Grapevine: Volunteerism's Newsletter.*

"GRAPEVINE: Volunteerism's Newsletter" & "Grapevine EXTRA!"

"How Volunteer Program Executives and Leaders keep up-to-date on fast-breaking news, information, resources and concerns."

People who lead volunteer programs in the public, private or independent sectors have come to depend on **GRAPEVINE** and **Grapevine EXTRA!** as their best source of information to help them meet the challenges of their jobs.

GRAPEVINE, started on its way in 1981 by Founding Editor Sue Vineyard, comes 6 times each year, with its 16 pages full of practical information you can use immediately. Written by Sue and co-editor Steve McCurley, it offers:

☞ **"News You Can Use"**: Up to date news that affects volunteerism.... legislation, concerns, mergers, conferences, liability issues, etc..

☞ **"Along the Vine"**: News from and about people in our field, job openings, tips, etc.

☞ **"Management"**: Full length, instructive articles on how to manage people and work; i.e.: Recognition, Climate, How to Fire Volunteers, ADA Compliance, Training, Supervision, Evaluation, Change, etc.

☞ **"DOVIA EXCHANGE"**: a newsletter within the vine for DOVIAs across N. America; written by contributing Editor, Ivan Scheier, Ph.D.

☞ **"Resources"**: New books, computer programs, recognition items, catalogs, etc.

☞ **Book Reviews**: A peek at the latest offerings for our field.

☞ **Lead Stories** offering in-depth information on the biggest stories for our field: National Service, Organizational mergers & changes, Volunteers impact on natural disasters, OSHA demands effecting volunteer programs, Legal cases, etc..

.... plus lots and lots of lists, tidbits and even a drop or two of humor to brighten your day!

Subscribe today: just $22 for an annual subscription.

Grapevine EXTRA! is the bi-monthly newsletter supplement that comes BETWEEN issues of GRAPEVINE to bring you fast-breaking news that can't wait! (Available to Grapevine subscribers only!) *6 issues a year: $10.*
(Subscription form on following page)

"Volunteer MARKETPLACE" Catalog

Offering Books, Monographs, Videos, Audios, Training Tools, Newsletters.....& more!

Books:

101 Ideas for Volunteer Programs
101 Tips for Volunteer Recruitment
101 Ways to Raise Resources
Essential Volunteer Management
Recruiting Volunteers for Difficult & Long Term Assignments
Volunteer Management Forms
Volunteer Management Policies
Marketing Magic for Volunteer Programs
Evaluating Volunteers, Programs & Events
Secrets of Motivation: How to Get & Keep Volunteers!
Secrets of Leadership
How to Take Care of You, So You Can Take Care of Others
The Great Trainers Guide: How to Train (almost) Anyone to do (almost) Anything!
Beyond Banquets, Plaques & Pins: Creative Ways to Recognize Volunteers
Managing Volunteer Diversity
Lead!
Developing Your Leadership Potential
Leadership Skills for the New Age of Nonprofits
We Can't Keep Meeting Like This!
Curing Terminal Niceness: Positive Volunteer-Staff Relations
Dealing With Difficult Volunteers
Building Credibility With the Powers That Be
Communications: A Positive Message From You
Change: Meet It and Greet It
Getting To Yes In Fund Raising
Megatrends & Volunteerism: Mapping the Future of Volunteer Programs
Volunteer Development Toolbox
The Group Member's Handbook
What If..A Guide to Ethical Decision Making
How to Control Liability & Risk in Volunteer Programs
Constructive Conflict

Other Items:

Audios: Preventing Burnout; Care for the Caregiver; Making Peace With Yourself; Fear of Fighting.

Video: Basic Volunteer Management: Building a Bridge from Dream to Reality.

Training Aides: Basic Volunteer Management Training Kit; Case Studies for Training Volunteers; Case Studies for Training Board Members.

Newsletters: GRAPEVINE: Volunteerism's Newsletter; Grapevine EXTRA!

Write for Free Catalog: Volunteer Marketplace, 1807 Prairie Ave., Downers Grove, IL 60515.

WANT TO MAKE MONEY AT YOUR CONFERENCE? We offer a consignment plan where you sell our products and retain 20% of sales. No up-front money from you. Simple. Effective. Productive! FAX a request for the Conference Consignment Plan Information Packet: FAX #: (708) 964-7338.

One Stop shopping for Everything You Need in Volunteerism:

Subscription Form:

☐ **I want to subscribe to GRAPEVINE ($22)** 6 issues per year.

☐ **Grapevine EXTRA! ($10, for Grapeviners only) at least 6 times per year.**

Name: _____Dept:_____

Organization: _____Phone: _____

Address: _____

City: _____State: _____ Zip: _____

Send check or money order to:
Grapevine, 1807 Prairie Ave., Downers Grove, IL 60515 or
FAX order and we will bill you: (708) 964-7338 (FAX orders received 24 hrs. a day.)